Leadership PQ

For Dorothy Caddell, and in memory of Andrew Caddell,
Josephine and Gerald Reffo

Leadership PQ

How political intelligence sets successful leaders apart

Gerry Reffo
and Valerie Wark

KoganPage

LONDON PHILADELPHIA NEW DELHI

First published in Great Britain and the United States in 2014 by Kogan Page Limited

2nd Floor, 45 Gee Street
London EC1V 3RS
United Kingdom

1518 Walnut Street, Suite 1100
Philadelphia PA 19102
USA

4737/23 Ansari Road
Daryaganj
New Delhi 110002
India

www.koganpage.com

© Gerry Reffo and Valerie Wark, 2014

The right of Gerry Reffo and Valerie Wark to be identified as the author of this work has been asserted by them in accordance with the Copyright, Designs and Patents Act 1988.

ISBN   978 0 7494 6960 3
E-ISBN   978 0 7494 6961 0

British Library Cataloguing-in-Publication Data

A CIP record for this book is available from the British Library.

Library of Congress Cataloging-in-Publication Data

Reffo, Gerry.
    Leadership PQ : how political intelligence sets successful leaders apart / Gerry Reffo, Valerie Wark.
      pages cm
    Includes index.
      ISBN 978-0-7494-6960-3 – ISBN 978-0-7494-6961-0 (ebk) 1. Leadership – Political aspects.
2. Business and politics. 3. Strategic alliances (Business) I. Wark, Valerie. II. Title.
    HD57.7.R443 2014
    658.4'092–dc23

                                                                      2013049648

Typeset by AMNET
Print production managed by Jellyfish
Printed and bound in by CPI group (UK) Ltd, Croydon CR0 4YY

CONTENTS

PART TWO The PQ model 39

LIST OF FIGURES

LIST OF TABLES

FOREWORD

Whether they work in government or business most of today's leaders cut their teeth in a different world. One where the best recipe for successful enterprise seemed to be for governments to provide a stable, market-oriented regulatory regime, and allow companies to get on with the business of creating economic growth.

Nationalized companies, or those with close ties to governments, were less successful than those subject to the discipline of shareholder scrutiny and market forces. Privatization went hand in hand with economic renaissance. The companies who thrived were those who kept away from the world of electoral politics with its short-term compromises, and focused instead on the business basics: efficient process, technology, financial discipline, marketing flair and customers.

The job of government was to get out of the way.

Much has changed, both in the way governments govern, and in the attitudes of government to business. The underlying thesis of this book – that leaders must find better ways to enable business, government and society to work together to deliver profit, growth, and better lives for future generations – reflects those changes.

The first of those changes is the development of a different kind of politics.

In emerging economies and developing countries, as well as in the established post-industrial democracies, the social media are subverting orthodox, traditional political process. Mass movements, organized at short notice, and often without any coherent political programme, have been able to unseat governments (Egypt, 2013) or turn public opinion upside down in just a few short weeks (Brazil, 2013).

The Chinese leadership are sensitive to online opinion, and Western governments monitor the digital space to see where the next story is coming from, and to prepare their response. Governments are learning that issues can come of out nowhere to dominate the political agenda. That agenda has become much harder to control.

The disenfranchised or disillusioned can mobilize and organize independent of established parties, and in hours or days rather than weeks or months.

Alongside that, access to education and to the information available on the Web – from anywhere in the world, about anywhere in the world – has increased the expectations of the governed.

And the governments who must meet those expectations are often at a loss as they wrestle to reconcile conflicting objectives: economic growth with environmental stewardship, a competitive economy with a compassionate society, fear of international entanglement and the dangers of isolationism. The dilemmas are not new – but the dynamic of modern politics makes them more intractable.

So, governments everywhere are unpredictable. Business and the press lament the lack of political leaders and blame today's politicians. But they confuse cause and effect. The new democracy of the internet age has sacrificed consistent long-term policy to the demands of the pressure groups. Political legitimacy is now made as much online or in the streets as at elections. That is the world we all live in.

But there is more to it than the Internet. Public attitudes to business changed with Great Financial Crisis. Until then wealth acquisition and wealth creation seemed to be the same. Many governments were ready to vouch for business, which would provide the economic growth to support the public policies and win elections. Today's voters have a different view, not just of bankers but of business in general. The public is now sceptical of their motives and of their conduct, and suspects that they pursue their own interests and that of their shareholders at the expense of society as a whole.

What's more, much of the world, in particular the fast-growing emerging economies, simply does not apply, or even accept, the market-led, open competition orthodoxy of the 80s and 90s. In Asia, or Russia, or Latin America, the ties between business and government are complex and close. Business decisions may be pure business decisions, but other factors may be in play. Governments in much of the world have never accepted that their job was to get out of the way. And that is unlikely to change.

Companies cannot take for granted a predictable investment climate. Business must create its own legitimacy, independent of government, and corporates must develop a deep, first-hand understanding of local and national politics as the basis for its investment decisions.

The skills required to be a brilliant engineer, geologist, trader or marketer are not the skills of the political world. Commercial acumen or entrepreneurial flair often jar with the manoeuverings of government or the complex objectives of long-term public policy. It is always tempting, when that happens, to hanker after the simpler days when business was business, government was government, and each was left to its own.

The best companies know, however, that business must deal with the world as it is, not as it would like it to be.

Companies should train their emerging leaders to work with the new political reality and give them the experience and expertise to make their dealings with politicians an integral part of their approach to business. Government should train their emerging leaders to work with business and wider society because together they might find innovative and effective long-term solutions to society's most intractable dilemmas.

This book was written in that spirit. I hope it is widely read.

Sir John Grant KCMG
Executive Vice President,
Policy and Corporate Affairs
BG Group

ACKNOWLEDGEMENTS

We were only able to write this book because of the generosity of the following leaders who shared their experience and expertise with us. They're all exceptionally busy people, yet they were generous enough to make time to help us and to talk about what they believe in.

US

Jeff Bewkes, Chairman and CEO, Time Warner.

Judy Brown, Head of Stakeholder Engagement, Rio Tinto.

Alexander Evans, Senior official, United Nations, academic and diplomat.

Muhtar Kent, Chairman and CEO of The Coca-Cola Company.

Adrian Paull, Vice President, Customer and Product Support, Honeywell Aerospace.

Nancy Beer Tobin, Assistant Dean, Georgetown Business School.

Sir Peter Westmacott, British Ambassador to the US.

Bob Zoellick, former Head of the World Bank and US Trade Envoy.

UK

Julian Braithwaite, UK Ambassador to the EU Political and Security Committee.

Conrad Bird, Director, the GREAT Britain Campaign, No 10 Downing Street.

Vicky Bowman, Director The Myanmar Centre for Responsible Business. Former Global Practice Leader, External Affairs, Rio Tinto.

Sir Kim Darroch, UK National Security Adviser.

Andrew Dunnett, Group Director, Sustainability and the Vodafone Foundation.

Hugh Elliott, Director Communications and Engagement, UK Foreign Office. Former Head of External Affairs, Anglo American plc.

David Frost, CEO Scotch Whiskey Association. Former International Director, UK Ministry for Business. Innovation and Skills (BIS).

Joe Garner, CEO, BT Openreach. Former Head of HSBC UK Retail Bank and Deputy CEO, HSBC Bank PLC

Brendan Gormley, Chair CDAC Network. Former CEO, UK Disasters Emergency Committee.

Sir John Grant, Executive Vice President, Policy and Corporate Affairs, BG Group.

Lord Green, Minister of State for Trade and Investment. Former Group Chairman HSBC Holdings PLC.

Peter Hawkins, author, academic and executive coach.

Peter Hayes, senior diplomat, former Head of Public Affairs, London Stock Exchange and British High Commissioner to Sri Lanka.

Dame Denise Holt, Non-Executive Director on various boards including HSBC Bank plc. Former British Ambassador to Spain.

Lord Jay, Chairman, Merlin Humanitarian Agency. Non-Executive Director, EDF Energy. Former Head of UK Foreign Office.

Lord Kerr, Deputy Chairman, Scottish Power. Former Deputy Chairman Shell, British Ambassador to the United States, and Head of UK Foreign Office.

Matthew Kirk, Group External Affairs Director, Vodafone.

Dominic Martin, G8 co-ordinator, UK Cabinet Office.

Mark Pegg, CEO Leadership Foundation for Higher Education.

Kai Peters, CEO Ashridge Business School.

Andrew Pike, Deputy Director, the GREAT Britain Campaign, No 10 Downing Street.

Edmond Rose, Director of Airline Planning, Virgin Atlantic.

Matthew Rycroft, Chief Operating Officer, British Foreign Office.

Guy Salter, Luxury brands expert. Chair of Walpole Crafted, member of the Prince's Trust Council.

Mark Sedwill, Permanent Secretary, UK Home Office. Former NATO Civilian Representative in Afghanistan.

We would also like to thank our editor, Liz Gooster, for her encouragement, advice and support; Michael Roberts, for his rigorous analysis and invaluable advice; Nancy Wallace for getting the manuscript into shape; and Paul Waller for his incredibly helpful eagle-eyed review. We're also grateful to others who freely gave their time to read and comment on chapters Jim Cannon, Catherine Morris and Dan Tarshish.

We'd like to thank Aldo Brazza for the illustrations and graphic content; Toby Roe, Jenny Murray and Chris Johnson of Ashridge for their generous help and advice on marketing and communications.

Finally, we'd like to thank our families for their encouragement and support throughout. Brian, Helen, Iona and Hannah Wark, and Elaine and Brian Cooper.

PART ONE
Introducing political intelligence (PQ)

What is PQ and why does it matter?

Out of the confusion, complexity and challenge of today emerges an opportunity to lead differently tomorrow.

Why it matters

The future demands leaders who can do more. The new leadership challenge is to deliver profit growth and a better future by business, government and society working together.

Globalization, complex societal challenges, changes in the planet, population, wealth and technology mean that the world is becoming more interdependent and power is more broadly distributed. It's happening now and it will intensify.

Business, government and non-profit sectors affect each other through the things they do and don't do. They also need each other because they cannot deliver alone. Leaders in all sectors operate within this relationship of shared power. Adjusting to it means that they have to do things differently. Some are better at it than others.

What are the best leaders and the most successful organizations doing? They look beyond the urgent and immediate day-to-day demands to see what the future needs and how that shapes what they do today. What they find is complex and multi-dimensional. Dealing with it requires intense focus and the capacity to work with multiple stakeholders and partners. Likely solutions are long term, innovative and benefit all.

How do they do this? Using most of the skills you might expect: cognitive intelligence (IQ) and emotional intelligence (EQ). But there is more to it. It's a different form of intelligence. We've called it Political Intelligence (PQ). PQ draws on both IQ and EQ and extends beyond them both. Here is our definition:

> PQ is the leadership capacity to interact strategically in a world where government, business and wider society share power to shape the future in a global economy.

You might wonder why we've used the term 'political' intelligence. We've returned to the Greek origin of the word politics. It is *politikos*, meaning of or relating to citizens: civic. PQ is rooted in the relationship between citizens, government and business.

This book describes the skills, behaviours and processes required to lead effectively when power is shared and the objective is to deliver profit for business and social benefits for wider society. We know that leaders in all sectors are exceptionally busy and want tools that are useable. So, we've designed a simple model of PQ leadership capacity based on five facets. We've also included help for individuals to develop their own PQ. For senior leaders, we've offered tools and methodology for implementing PQ in your organization.

Our book is intensely practical. It's written for leaders and future leaders in all sectors. We share with you practical advice and examples from successful leaders. We've focused on the best in class. In business, this means leaders of organizations that combine (huge) profit with an active contribution to society. In public policy and non-profit organizations, it means showing how partnership works to deliver impact and scale. We've also invited leaders with senior level experience of business and government to contribute.

What we describe is not easy to master, so this book is for the courageous. We want it to inspire leaders in all sectors and in all sizes of organization to challenge themselves and their colleagues about what they do, how they do it, and how they might do it better.

Who needs PQ?

If you are a leader, or want to be a leader, then PQ is for you. It is targeted at:

- business leaders at multinational and local level;
- leaders involved in public policy and delivery;
- leaders of non-profit organizations;
- executive teams;
- aspiring leaders in all sectors.

While we acknowledge that each sector faces different challenges, we've found a common denominator that successful leaders and successful organizations share. PQ gives them reach and impact because they work with others to deliver more in the broadest sense.

What PQ isn't

We should say here what PQ and this book is not about. It's not a guide to politics, nor is it a manual to help you navigate internal organizational politics.

You might be wondering – is this simply about working in a collaborative way? What's new in it? How will it benefit me?

First, let's be clear. Collaborative working is ongoing, important and essential. We're not questioning that. But PQ is more than working together with one or more people to achieve a purpose.

What PQ is

PQ is for leaders with enough insight, vision and humility to recognize that they are working within a wider system. What they offer has to meet the needs of customers, consumers, citizens, the environment and future generations. No one sector or organization can deliver what is needed alone. Government, business and society share the power to provide better outcomes for all.

Why has the need for PQ arisen?

In the 1980s and 1990s in many developed economies there was a widespread view that government had proved pretty useless at trying to manage the economy. The consequence had been poor economic growth. The solution was that government adapted its role in the management of the economy to providing a stable long-term macro-economic framework and a stable regulatory climate (not too much regulation and not too little), allowing business to get on with making money.

Taxes would then allow government to do its other job, which was the provision of public services. Most business leaders at the top of companies today cut their teeth in this world.

The world is different now. Most businesses don't operate in a stable long-term economy, nor do they have the regulatory environment they want. The world is becoming more regulated. And few countries would be described by business as 'well governed', with the promise of predictable business-friendly policies.

We asked Sir John Grant, Executive Vice President Policy and Corporate Affairs at BG Group and a former top diplomat, for a business view of government. He observed the following:

- Electorates/citizens are better educated, better informed, better networked and as a result better organized and more demanding than ever before.

- Governments face greater constraints than ever before, largely as a result of globalization which puts international capital in control and reduces governments' room for manoeuvre and has created a whole set of problems which governments can't solve by themselves (climate change, immigration being two).

The result is that democratic governments are generally in thrall to the news cycle and have to react all the time to developments outside their control. This gives enormous influence to minorities and makes it almost inevitable that governments will pursue short-term and unpredictable policies which business won't like.

Moises Naim, a former Venezuelan trade and industry minister and editor in chief of *Foreign Policy* magazine, comes from a different background to John but reaches a similar conclusion. In his book

The End of Power (2013), he argues that all leaders (including political, business and military) face bigger and more complex problems. Why? He cites three 'Ms':

- *more* of everyone and everything, which overwhelms the means of control;
- greater *mobility* of people and ideas; and
- a new *mentality* bringing different aspirations, expectations and values.

The impact of the three 'Ms' is felt by leaders in government, business and non-profit organizations. Those who exercise power are more constrained and less secure than their predecessors across the board. Government struggles with the speed of ideas and change. By trying to please all, politicians can miss the need to lead and govern.

Business struggles with the speed in which reputations of companies, products and services change. Partly, this is because of greater transparency and partly because consumer values, perceptions and expectations evolve.

Non-profit organizations benefit when their cause is aligned with the public mood, but struggle if public sympathy shifts. The UK charity regulator, the Charity Commission (2012), aware of the risks, recently warned about large executive pay increases when donations to charities are going down, bringing the wider charitable sector into disrepute.

So what is the challenge for today's leaders?

The task facing today's leaders is how to lead in a world where government cannot govern alone and the world is facing complex global challenges.

Muhtar Kent, Chairman and CEO of The Coca-Cola Company, has thought deeply about this question. He says: 'Government can't do it alone. For capitalism to thrive, it has to connect all stakeholders and not just shareholders.' Muhtar describes it as a 'Golden Triangle'. The Golden Triangle connects government, business and civil society (see Figure 1.1).

FIGURE 1.1 The Golden Triangle

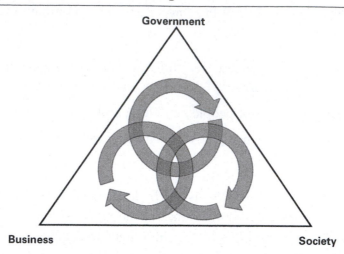

Sir Richard Branson has similar ideas about the need for business to do more to help society. Talking to Bloomberg TV, Branson suggested that if business leaders worldwide were to adopt a social problem and use their business and entrepreneurial skills to tackle it, most problems would be solved.

Political leaders share a similar perspective. Former President Bill Clinton in his Nomination Speech supporting President Obama in September 2012 said: 'We think the country works better with business and government actively working together to promote growth and broadly shared prosperity.' David Cameron, UK Prime Minister, said in 2012: 'Business is not just about making money, as vital as that is; it's the most powerful force for making social progress the world has ever known.'

We explored with Muhtar his belief that the complex issues facing the world have to be addressed from within the 'Golden Triangle'. He told us that business leaders must search for 'multiple solutions to multiple problems' and deliver 'better outcomes' for customers, consumers and government – both national and local.

We recognize that for many leaders in government and business this approach will not be usual. They've grown up with the belief that government governs and business makes money. The two don't often cross over. We asked Muhtar why he felt differently.

He answered as a parent and then as a businessman. Speaking as a parent and referring to all it takes to preserve our planet's fragile economy, he said: 'I want my children to be able to eat fresh fish.'

Speaking, as the head of a $14bn global corporation and one of the best-known brands on the planet, he said: 'There is a hard business outcome hanging in the balance. Consumers want to know and understand *the character of a company*. If there is a big gap between public expectation and reality, you're in trouble.'

Jeff Bewkes, Chairman and CEO of Time Warner, suggested to us that we compare the traditional business models, where profit increases by improving efficiency and economy of scale, with the new network model. Pointing to Google as an example, Jeff explains that consumers search Google online. The searches tell Google what content users want. Google responds and in so doing provides a better product. The better product attracts more users.

Here's the point: *profit is driven by interaction with and between consumers/society* and that gives consumers more influence with business because the individual consumers not only make their own choice about whether to buy or not, they also influence others' choices. And those choices are driven by both *product quality* and as Muhtar Kent puts it *'the character of the company'*.

Shared value

Michael Porter and Mark Kramer wrote a prescient piece in the *Harvard Business Review* (January/February 2011) about how business and government need to change. They called it 'Creating shared value'.

For companies, it's about doing things that enhance their competitiveness and improve the economic and social conditions in the communities in which they operate. Porter and Kramer say:

A narrow conception of capitalism has prevented business from harnessing its full potential to meet society's broader challenges. *Businesses acting as businesses, not as charitable donors, are the most powerful force for addressing the pressing issues we face.*

Society's needs are large and growing, while customers, employees and a new generation of young people are asking business to step up.

The purpose of the corporation must be to create shared value. This will drive the next wave of innovation and productivity growth in the global economy. It will also reshape capitalism and its relationship to society. Perhaps most important of all, learning how to create shared value is our best chance to legitimize business again.

Porter and Kramer insist that 'shared value' is not about philanthropy but self-interest. And Muhtar Kent also asserts that there must be a hard business outcome. So, whether we call it working in the Golden Triangle (a term we love) or creating shared value, the emphasis is on mutual benefit. And, it's different from philanthropy, donations, volunteering or other corporate social responsibility activities.

How it works

Non-profit

Many non-profit organizations recognize that they need a broader partnership to achieve their aims. The international NGO Save the Children is upfront about what it needs from business. 'Without business, we will not solve these complex development challenges, their involvement is critical to our success.'

Save the Children Fund is asking businesses to do the following:

- apply a 'do no harm' approach to their core business;
- shape core business strategies to contribute to development goals;
- advocate change at a national and global level.

Business

In the following example, business works to solve one of society's most pressing problems. Virgin Atlantic's business is air travel and it knows that people enjoy travel. So rather than tell people to travel less, it's working on a solution that makes the planet safer, allows people to travel and maintains its core business.

CASE STUDY Private sector

Virgin Atlantic – sustainable aviation

Vision

Sir Richard Branson's vision for Virgin Atlantic is to be the leading airline on sustainability, driving solutions for the whole industry by developing sustainable fuels for commercial use on Virgin Atlantic aircraft. He's set the challenging target of a 30 per cent reduction in emissions by 2020. He understands how important it is for the planet to cut carbon emissions and he is doing something about it.

Innovation

In New Zealand, a small innovative company called LanzaTech was formed when one of the founders (Dr Sean Simpson) noticed that steel production waste gases were being burnt into the atmosphere as carbon dioxide and he thought the waste could be used as aviation fuel. He built a small factory and set about proving it.

Partnership

In 2008, Virgin formed a partnership with LanzaTech with the goal of developing the world's first low-carbon aviation fuel.

Power and resources

Branson has committed all profits made by Virgin Atlantic to developing cleaner fuel. Jennifer Holmglen, CEO of Lanzatech, says 'Innovative technologies don't commercialise themselves; rather they're commercialised through investment and co-ordination with forward looking companies like Virgin Atlantic.'

Focus

Richard Branson explains it best in one of his blogs: 'Whenever you try something radically different it takes a lot of time and testing for it to be accepted. The important thing is to keep chasing ground breaking solutions.'

Character of the company

Virgin Atlantic tells consumers that it will take responsibility for the environmental impact of aviation. Its stance contrasts with many US airlines who've opted out of a European Commission plan to reduce aviation carbon emissions. Virgin, in contrast, joined the EU emissions trading scheme in early 2012. Stephen King (general manager, Virgin-India) says: 'We're known as a company that cares about what we do and how we do it.'

Business outcome?

And yes, just like Coca-Cola, there's a hard business outcome too. Stephen King points out: 'We know that sustainability can offer us a triple win – for example achieving fuel, energy, carbon reductions and reducing use of materials can save us money and makes good business sense, but it's also simply the right thing to do.'

Delivery

The prize-winning partnership plans to move into commercial-level production of aviation fuel in 2014.

(Virgin Atlantic, 2013)

Business/non-profit/government

In the next example, an NGO, business and government team up to deliver a good outcome for people.

CASE STUDY   The last mile

The Global Fund, supported by the Gates Foundation, teamed up with Coca Cola and the government of Tanzania to improve the supply chain for medicines. The problem was how to deliver HIV/AIDS, tuberculosis, malarial and other medicines and supplies to remote villages. While a bottle of Coke can be found everywhere, essential medicines are not always able to get through.

Two years after the project began, 120 essential medicines are being delivered to 5,000 health facilities, instead of only 500. Even better, the typical delivery time has been reduced from 30 days to 5 days, a difference that is likely to save a lot of lives. Overall, almost 20 million people – nearly half the population of Tanzania – have access to those health facilities.

Direct delivery also allows better information flow, so that health officials better understand how medicines reach health clinics, and which health facilities are operating well and which are not, improving planning, logistics and stock management. And public sector staff are learning first-hand about business solutions from the private sector.

To build on this success, the project is being expanded to Ghana and Mozambique. Muhtar Kent reflected that, because of his company's distribution systems, Coca-Cola could help reach the last mile in Africa'.

International integration

Everything is becoming more integrated, both nationally and internationally. Business and government work within an international system that regulates a broad range of issues from trade to employment, from international waters to environmental targets.

The OECD (2012) predicted that China is likely to take over from the United States as the world's largest economy in the following few years. India has replaced Japan as the third largest economy. Moves towards closer integration are visible as the world adapts to changes in economic power. South East Asia and Latin America have set up organizations to help them develop closer trading and economic ties. Europe and the United States are negotiating a transatlantic trade agreement.

More integration requires more multilateral government activity on all significant issues – financial, economic, trade, climate, migration etc. It also means more international regulation that business will have to understand and adopt.

Sharing infrastructure and services

Reflecting the trend for working together, the PwC 16th Annual Survey of Global CEOs (2013) reported that businesses are looking much more at collaboration with adjacent industries to share infrastructure and co-develop products. Why? To reduce risk and bring costs down in areas like research and development. It's also more economic than traditional approaches such as merger or acquisition.

How should business leaders respond?

First, business leaders must understand this more complex 'political' environment. It's not sufficient to rely on government to create a business-friendly environment and operate inside it. Businesses need to be able to work with government to:

- anticipate where the problems are coming from;
- exert as much influence on the political world as the campaigning NGOs, Twitter campaigns and media stories that dictate so much of modern government; and
- become part of the solution, rather than one of the problems.

The best business leaders of the future will think about how they can help government strike a balance between responding to the short term and encouraging long-term strategic policies and businesses.

Critical to success is the understanding that business is part of a wider societal system and that society expects them to step up to the mark. Forward-thinking leaders take opportunities to do business in a way that positively impacts society because they're part of society and it makes good business sense.

Isn't this what public affairs professionals do?

Traditionally business has relied on public affairs/external affairs specialists to help them engage with government. The requirement for this in-depth professional expertise not only remains, but is growing because of political, regulatory and societal changes.

Interest in public policy and wider societal issues now engages a widening group of stakeholders. Business has to respond by developing broader communications strategies to meet this demand. More international regulation means that companies must have a globally coherent policy as well as understanding the national and regional context of the countries they operate in. Research into how public affairs is changing (Watson Helsby, 2011) identified more involvement in strategy and business planning, reflecting the growing impact of political and regulatory issues.

The need for a more integrated working relationship between government and business to tackle the big challenges at various levels means that it's no longer enough to have one or two politically intelligent leaders at the top of a business and to rely on public affairs expertise to get the other leaders through.

A globally connected and interdependent world brings with it complex stakeholder relationships including local and national governments, citizens and communities, media, NGOs, shareholders, unions and employees. The consequence of this is that those responsible for business in foreign countries – CEOs and divisional heads – those responsible for design and development of new products, those leading on finance, tax and corporate responsibility, and all those with executive functions on the main board and non-executives have to exercise politically intelligent leadership.

Global companies like Rio Tinto and Vodafone are training their senior leaders to understand their role in this complex environment. Sir John Grant observes that 'the next generation of business leaders will have to think like businessmen as well as being able to put themselves into the shoes of politicians'.

How should leaders in government respond?

Today's public policy officials were brought up with a strong belief in service, but that got mixed up because of the 24/7 media hubbub and pressure from politicians to be seen to respond. The outcome, mainly in democracies, is too much focus on the short term and a growing gap between rhetoric and delivery. This is not popular among the electorate, who may not know the policy detail but instinctively recognize when they're being played and become disengaged.

Government officials are core to the political machine of government and mainly responsible for policy delivery. Generally, officials interact with business only when they want something. Attitudes must shift if the vision of former President Clinton of 'government and business actively working together' is to be realized.

Most senior government and public sector leaders, across all policy areas from social policy to foreign affairs to infrastructure development, face a challenge of upgrading leadership skills in their organizations. Too often, working with business or non-profit sectors is seen as a way to reduce cost and the public sector workforce. The opportunity to create innovative and long-term solutions is lost. Government must learn how to work with business more intelligently.

Porter and Kramer suggest more focus on the results achieved rather than the funds and efforts expended. The economic recession and increase in debt complicate this because there is less money to spend and more focus on value. In 2014, the focus must be on the results and achieving them efficiently and economically.

Bob Zoellick, former Head of the World Bank and US Trade Envoy, spoke with conviction about the importance of delivery in public policy: 'Many public officials seem content to hold posts, be part of the flow of events, analyse and comment and attend meetings.' He stresses the importance of delivering results: 'the challenge to the public sector is to continue to focus on getting things done.'

Some might legitimately feel that the points about getting things done have been around for a long time. It's true, they have. But they remain valid. Business leaders who work with government told us, repeatedly, that business is more focused on delivery.

The challenge facing leaders in government is how to manage a wide range of multi-dimensional public policies involving multiple stakeholders so that they deliver better long-term outcomes for society.

So, if the argument holds that the next generation of business people will need to put themselves in the shoes of politicians, then the next generation of public policy leaders must acquire some of the skills of business.

How should non-profit leaders respond?

The non-profit world is large and diverse. In most cases it has the ear of government in a way that business does not. The large charities meet with government regularly. The smaller ones are tied into local communities and local government. The large international institutions and global foundations have mostly unlimited access to whoever they want to see and to national media.

The future dictates that government and non-profits must work together to deliver services and to shape a better future. Government brings power and an opportunity to move forward, but non-profits must not allow too much short termism as politicians aim to deliver a good news story within the electoral cycle.

Politics is intoxicating to be around. But too much politics and non-profits may lose public trust. Non-profit leaders need political skills to help navigate through these difficult waters.

The large humanitarian agencies have their PQ skills fully tested when they are forced to deal with brutal regimes in the interest of saving lives. The best examples are a source of education to all leaders.

What is noticeable is the rise, in recent years, of the mega-large non-profits such as the Gates Foundation and the Clinton Foundation. Their focus is on very clear outcomes, long-term results and delivery. The public notice this. Social media savvy, these big foundations engage citizens worldwide in their activities.

Smaller non-profits may find more questions asked about long-term delivery and concrete outcomes from their activities as comparisons are made. Scrutiny of their operations will increase from both government donors and citizen donors – both asking questions about cost effectiveness because of competing causes for available money.

The PQ model

We've created a PQ leadership model that describes the behaviours, skills and processes that, used in harmony, comprise Politically Intelligent leadership (PQ leadership). We explore these in a business and government context. What may surprise you is that the behaviours, skills and processes are universal and apply across sectors. Leaders who have high levels of PQ stand out as successful in all fields. We explore these in detail in Part Two.

Our conclusions on PQ leadership capacity are based on interviews with leaders in multinational companies and in government, and with leaders who have worked in both worlds. They've shared their thinking and experience with us. We've added to this by drawing on open source material when appropriate and drawing in corroborative examples from other leaders who act with political intelligence.

We've found out what some of the best leaders are doing. We believe this flags the path for other leaders. Drawing on our own experience of coaching senior leaders, executive education and human resource management, we've designed a model that we hope you will find useful.

How could PQ make a difference?

We've considered the challenges and the changes in leadership that are required. To put this into context, we've mapped out what PQ leadership looks like for business, government and society. Table 1.1 describes:

- fundamental challenges facing each stakeholder group;
- the type of solutions they must generate;
- the outcomes for each stakeholder group; and
- the ultimate beneficiaries.

What we noticed is that the solutions share similar characteristics. The most common characteristics are:

- *Innovative*: complex problems won't be solved by existing practices.
- *International*: significant change needs international co-operation.
- *Long term*: meaningful change requires time to embed.
- *Sustainable*: maintain essential resources.
- *Ethical*: people need trust in leaders to commit to change.

TABLE 1.1 PQ Leadership Map

Stakeholders	Challenges	Characteristics of the solutions	Better stakeholder outcomes	Beneficiaries
Government	• More complexity • Less control • Less resource • Immediate judgement by 24/7 media • Loss of citizen confidence	• International solutions • Innovative solutions • Long-term solutions • Viable solutions • Partnership	• Societal progress • Longevity • Legitimacy • Stability	• Citizens • Future generations
Business	• Unsustainable products and services • More scrutiny • Higher consumer expectations • Consumer power	• Creative solutions • Ethical solutions • Reputation enhancement • Long-term solutions • Partnership	• Profit • Longevity • Legitimacy • Value	• Shareholders • Employees • Customers • Consumers
Society	• Climate • Resource availability • Security • Equality • Corporate and political excess	• Sustainable solutions • International agreements • Long-term solutions • Accountability • Ability to contribute	• Better lives • Better communities • Better futures	• Us • Our children • Future generations

It follows that the leaders whose focus is on delivering solutions with these characteristics are most likely to earn the trust and confidence of citizens, consumers and customers because they'll offer solutions to the big problems. Trust translates into loyalty at the ballot box and in the shopping basket.

Conclusion

PQ leadership is about finding better ways to enable business, government and society to work together to deliver profit, growth and better lives for future generations.

Dealing with multiple problems in a shared power world requires:

- ability to work comfortably with others across sector, cultural and international divides;
- focus on both profit and long-term societal benefits;
- long-term vision;
- innovation;
- ethics – valuing both the outcome and how it's achieved; and
- an open dialogue with society – two-way communication.

It's a shared power world

02

What is it?

A shared power world is one where no single organization is in full control of its destiny. Making profits, governing nations, providing public services and helping society are done more effectively when organizations work with others. Business, government and non-profit organizations raise their game when they embrace working with partners and stakeholders to achieve what they want individually and jointly.

The drivers underpinning change – politics, economics, sociological, technological advances and the environment – are all moving us further into mutual dependence. A narrow focus on product, services or policy, whether commercially or in government, is no longer enough. Leaders with the capacity to work in a shared power world and deliver better individual and joint outcomes are the new rock stars.

Jaded by a succession of leadership theories, you might ask: is this anything new? We suggest that the world is changing fast on almost every scale: shifting political and economic power; significant demographic change; digital communications; environmental threats and disasters. Perhaps most critical of all is the impact of globalization allied with digital and mobile technology. All of us know that we're more interconnected and more mutually dependent, but are we adapting fast enough?

Kishore Mahbubani, the former Singaporean diplomat and thought leader, argues (in his book *The Great Convergence*, 2013) that the prosperity and security of the rising and the economically advanced nations will depend on their ability *to share power*. He uses the analogy: we're all sailing on the same ship; our ability to stay afloat will depend on how we co-operate with each other, not on the size of our individual cabins.

Mahbubani's thesis for co-operation is compelling. But it rests on the ability of democratic leaders to convince their citizens that global interest trumps national interest. If John Grant is right (Chapter 1, page 6) that democratic governments, overly influenced by the news cycle and vociferous minorities, are deterred from acting in the long-term interest, then it's not only business that won't get the policies it wants, society won't get the policies it needs.

Change drivers

Thought leaders, authors and journalists draw attention to the drivers for environmental change. We'll cover some of their thinking below. A common theme is that government, business and international institutions must adapt the way they interact by finding better ways to share power. Broadening strategic objectives to extend beyond self/national interest is the first move.

Market failure

Many of today's top business leaders grew up with the belief that the phenomenon of globalization and the development of large multinational corporations would mean that national governments would become increasingly less influential. The global economic crisis and the apparent failure of the market to deliver prosperity in developed economies changed this.

In 2008, when the financial system was close to collapse, it was governments and central banks that stepped in to support the economy and to rescue failed banks. Power then shifted back towards government. The markets relied on politicians, central banks and financial institutions to provide the tools to deliver financial stability and encourage investor confidence. The exposure of mutual dependency between the market and governments has led to a more equal balance of power than many expected.

Despite this balance and efforts to better regulate markets, economies continue to be destabilized by the emphasis on short-term gains. *Time Magazine* reported (September 2013) that the entire value of the New York Stock Exchange turned over roughly every 12 months (that is, trading equalled the value of the stocks registered), a rate that has doubled since the 1990s.

Jim Galbraith, a University of Texas economist (quoted in the same article by Rana Foroohar) – says: '100 years of data shows that as asset investments rise, so too does inequality.' Inequality hurts society. The negative impact hits many businesses, jobs, standards of living and social stability.

Justin Welby, head of the Anglican Church, argues for 'the creation of a 21st century architecture for the financial services industry and banking sector, one which is ethical and profitable, innovative and safe'. Most citizens hit by the economic recession are likely to share his view. Governments' response is to regulate. But the real power to make it happen rests with the leaders of banks and financial services companies (Welby, 2013).

Wicked problems

Humanity has always faced problems. The 20th century brought two world wars, the Great Depression and nuclear stand-offs. The 21st century is no different in facing huge problems. They include climate change, resource scarcity, debt, inequality, poverty, disease, conflict, religious and ethnic intolerance.

What characterizes these problems is a multitude of causes: a historical legacy, a range of stakeholders with competing interests, and divided opinions on solutions.

Moving forward on any one of these problems requires compromises from major stakeholders, significant change and redistribution of resources. In fact, exactly the type of wider thinking Kishore Mahbubani advocates.

Demographics

World population is growing significantly: by 2050 it will reach between 8.1 billion with low fertility, and 10.6 billion with high fertility.

- *Increases in population* will put a premium on food, water and energy: a global population of around 8.3 billion people will need 35 per cent more food, 40 per cent more water and 50 per cent more energy.

- *Older people increase*: The number of people aged 50 or over will increase from 1.4 to 3.1 billion by 2050.

- *Rapid urbanization*: By 2025 the number of megacities (over 10 million inhabitants) will have increased to 37, with urban populations expected to grow to 6.3 billion.

- *Middle classes poised to grow* significantly in the next 15–20 years. Mainly in Asia and Africa.

- *Migration* will become more globalized as both rich and developing countries suffer from workforce shortages.

(Wilton Park Conference Report 2013: *Resources: trends and future challenges for states and regions – towards 2030* – www.wiltonpark. org.uk.)

Demographics

The profile of the world population is changing rapidly. The following statistics give you a flavour of anticipated changes in the next 30–40 years.

Demographic changes will make essential resources scarce. Most of the increase in world population will be in Africa, Asia and, to a lesser degree, Latin America. Economic development and rapid urbanization in the emerging economies is predicted to move 3 billion new people into the middle classes. Economic growth, improved education and political stability are potential benefits that ought to flow from this seismic shift. On the down side, natural resources will become scarcer.

Dambisa Moyo, a leading economist and author, explains that there are not enough commodity resources (land, water, energy, minerals) to support these trends, and the competition for scarce resources is pushing up prices and has potential to cause armed conflicts. China is very active in the regions that are rich in commodity resources.

Dambisa puts the case for a change of attitude in the West:

> There is still a reluctance to treat regions that traditionally have only been targets of aid, *as equal partners*. There has been one policy for developed and rapidly emerging markets and a completely different policy for Africa and other underdeveloped regions. The onus is on policymakers to encourage investment by setting a different tone (Nakagawa and Moyo, 2012).

Can government handle these changes alone? Sir John Grant, Executive Vice President Policy and Corporate Affairs at BG Group, pinpoints the drivers for a different relationship between government and business:

- 'Business and government find that problems which loosely relate to sustainability are only solved by working together.
- Government recognizes that if the market is not working then companies need to help to solve the problems caused by market failures.
- The world economy is conditioned by countries where government plays a significant role in commercial decision making, eg China, Russia.
- Trans-national problems dwarf government capability and business knows it.'

Struggling political systems

China's autocratic political system and state capitalism enable it to pursue and implement long-term policies and make short-term corrective changes quickly. It's ahead of the West, in having a systematic and strategic plan for securing scarce resources, investing in both Africa and other underdeveloped regions.

China is tackling internal inequality too. But it has yet to effectively challenge the corruption arising from the nature of the political system, such as a lack of political competition, little accountability, limited media freedom, and lack of confidence in the impartiality of the rule of law and judicial independence. Calls for freedom of expression are increasing and Chinese citizens are using social media to spread their message.

In the Western democratic system, private capitalism and the market form the economic platform. Politicians are in power for fixed terms and are accountable to the electorate. People enjoy freedom of expression and take for granted a free media, the rule of law and an independent judiciary.

Despite these strengths, governments struggle to govern effectively. Some parliaments are bi-partisan, others are multi-party. But neither system works that well. The electoral cycle encourages short ter-mism. Rana Foroohar (*Time Magazine*) comments on a low appetite for doing what is needed if it carries political risk. Since significant change, or indeed anything worthwhile, almost always involves risk, it is a bleak picture. The casualties are long-term coherent thinking, innovation and making a difference.

The London School of Economics Growth Commission (2013) summed up what doesn't work in the UK political system:

- policy failures (procrastination, reversals);
- short-term political horizons;
- adversarial politics causing tinkering, rebranding, reversals;
- lack of independent expert advice and evaluations;
- populist pressure.

This list could equally be applied to many if not most Western democracies. And, while society is the loser in this scenario, the addition of populist pressure in the list shows that it's also a contributor to what doesn't work. Social media-organized campaign groups apply more populist pressure than ever before. This is more democratic than behind the scenes lobbying and a force for good when opinion is well informed. But, it also has the capacity to undermine long-term societal reform when opinion is poorly informed.

International institutions

Political thought leaders are turning to international institutions as the way forward:

- Nicholas Berggruen and Nathan Gardels (2013), authors and thought leaders, warn that 'without political reforms that strengthen consensus-building practices and institutions that enable the long-term implementation of sustainable policies, democracies will fail'.

- Kishore Mahbubani suggests that today's leaders should build on multilateral institutions to encourage proud nations to think more globally.

If these deep thinkers are right, the onus will be on government leaders to develop laws, policies and regulations that not only meet the needs of their own citizens but are also compatible with the needs of a range of international partners. The challenge is both to work with others on mutually beneficial outcomes and to explain to the electorate why government must think beyond the 'size of its own cabin'.

The European Union

The EU is an example of successful international co-operation. Yet it continues to grapple with competing forces: the economic/trade benefits and political influence afforded by collectivism versus the demand for independent national decision making.

The EU project is one of the world's leading examples of international collaboration. It's a tribute to the political intelligence of post-war leaders that they designed a forum for European collaboration in 1956, which in 1993 evolved into the EU.

Despite nearly 60 years of co-operation, the European project now faces a central challenge on legitimacy, both for retaining the integration achieved so far and for extending integration further. This challenge comes from the different peoples of Europe expressed through their national states.

The EU has failed to become a single political community that would allow it to take on the attributes of statehood. Yet, economically, it needs more integration to support its single currency. Without more integration the survival of the euro is in question. Without the euro, Angela Merkel questions the survival of the EU.

Collaboration in Europe has achieved many successes over the years. We summarize the main ones below, together with some of the current challenges.

Example: international collaboration – the EU project

The successes

- A co-operative forum that enables EU countries to work together to resolve political differences.

- Has managed the competing interests and conflict that led to successive wars before its inception.

- Offers its members the biggest single trading market in the world.

- Collectively it's a political force in the world.

- Evolving through enlargement.

The challenges

- Legitimacy for further integration.

- Inspiring the peoples of Europe to support the EU.

- Inequality between nations and within nations.

- Bureaucracy and high administrative costs.

- Lack of competitiveness.

- Ageing populations.

- Institutional change.

How well the EU responds to challenges over legitimacy will depend on its capacity to win support from the peoples of Europe and an ability to change to meet new circumstances.

The United Nations

The UN is a symbol of how countries can work together and tackle the most difficult issues. Criticized at times for not doing enough, the UN inevitably faces some failures and setbacks because it deals with the most intractable problems and works with shared power decision-making mechanisms. Despite its independent status, in fact the UN has always been partial and political. Divided on issues, its membership reflects the diversity of world opinion and the nature of international co-operation.

Recognizing all of that, the UN is the most remarkable advert for shared power. It's a forum for discussion of world problems. It's saved hundreds of thousands of lives. It appears to have little political ego. UN leaders do not worry about taking political risks. Ready to go into the worst situations, they do so knowing that there are no easy wins and often the certainty of failure. They do it to save lives and without political posturing.

Current Security Council members are reluctant to cede power, but changes in the distribution of the world's political and economic power are moving the UN slowly towards new power sharing arrangements.

Reform

Finding solutions that offer good outcomes for society, business and national governments is a challenge. Securing the consensus necessary to design new political institutions or reform post-war international organizations to meet the demands of changing political and economic power is another.

Designing new structures that have membership buy-in and move the organizations forwards will demand high levels of political intelligence from the architects and their many political stakeholders.

Berggruen, Gardels and Mahbubani's solutions point towards more international co-operation. Facilitating this will require strong diplomacy and the skills of the best diplomats.

Wilton Park (2013), a UK-based forum for global change, calls for 'a new diplomacy'. Rather than just governments and diplomats, this involves multiple actors – sovereign states, business, social entrepreneurs, NGOs, academia, internet-based groups and individual citizens. An ambitious idea, it offers a radically different approach to international co-operation.

It poses a challenge to the world's diplomats to facilitate multilateral solutions with a more diverse cast of players who are not veterans of diplomatic protocols. It would be messy, but the potential for fresh thinking and innovation is exciting.

Regulation

Regulation and compliance issues were No 1 in the Top 10 risks in Ernst and Young's *Global Report* at the start of 2013. Brazil, France, the Middle East and the United States were identified as countries where the risk is highest. Banking and life sciences were the highest-risk sectors. In a 2013 PwC Survey, 50 per cent of global CEOs said government and regulators have significant influence on their business.

While business worries about too much regulation, citizens want more. Spurred on by disasters and mismanagement – such as: i) the financial crisis: a failure by regulators and business leaders; ii) the oil spill in the Gulf of Mexico: a failure by the industry, the company and the regulators, they've lost trust in business to sufficiently act in the public good.

Responding to the public mood, politicians are quicker to act than in the past. Publicly at least, they want distance between themselves and business on regulatory issues. While this improves objectivity, it is not the best way to get good regulation with only one party at the table.

Porter and Kramer in their *Harvard Business Review* article on 'Creating shared value' (discussed in Chapter 1) argue that the right kind of government regulation can encourage companies to invest in shared value. They define the characteristics of the right kind of regulation as:

- setting clear and measurable social goals;
- setting prices for resources that reflect true costs (when appropriate);
- setting performance standards but giving business flexibility to decide how to meet them;
- phasing in regulation to reflect the investment or new product cycle.

Leaders in government and business face the challenge of engaging in effective dialogue ahead of disasters to find the right balance of regulation in an international context. This is easier said than done. It demands the ability to:

- understand the whole system;
- anticipate risks;
- engage other partners in managing risk;
- make concessions and find consensus.

Applying regulation

Regulatory processes are more complex and internationally integrated, reflecting how industry works. Supply chains cross borders. Most businesses are exporting or importing goods. Consumers often don't know the origin of what they are buying, so they want to know that it's safe and that product descriptions are reliable. International regulation helps trade and gives consumers confidence in buying overseas products, but only if it works. See overleaf for an example of when it didn't.

People power

People's ability to collectively express their views both as consumers and voters is changing business and politics. Many organizations in all sectors are on the back foot in handling their own social media.

Political

The point of democracy is that all citizens should have an equal voice. Power has traditionally been exercised through the ballot box at elections. But many want their voices to be heard on issues that emerge between elections.

Social media enables collective sharing of information and opinions and has already had a major effect in engaging people with political issues. Governments have toppled. Policies have changed. Politicians in all forms of government are confronted with a new type of people power that has transparent communication at its core.

Horse meat sold as beef in the UK and Europe

In early 2013, it was discovered that some processed beef food dishes in fact contained horse meat (in volumes varying up to 100 per cent). The first discovery was in a British supermarket, but soon horse meat labelled as beef was found in a range of products produced and sold in Europe. Top brands were involved: Tesco (with horse-meat burgers), Findus (horse-meat lasagne), Nestle (horse-meat ravioli and lasagne) and Ikea (meatballs). All multinational brands.

The supply chain is multinational too. Figure 2.1 shows the journey of one product before it reached the shops.

FIGURE 2.1   The international supply chain

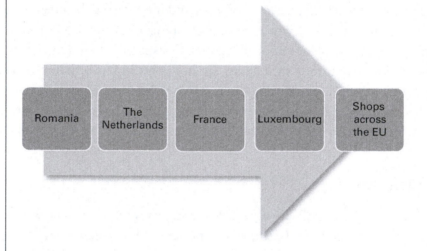

The horse-meat food chain shows how even making a lasagne becomes incredibly complex when the supply chain crosses international borders. What this story highlights is the importance of consistent application of regulations across international borders.

This is not easy to achieve. Four things need to be in place between national regulatory agencies, businesses and science:

- *integrity* in all parts of the system;

- *transparency* when things go wrong;

- *ability to co-operate* across countries;

- *a firm belief that all consumers matter* and deserve high standards not just those in your own country.

Thomas Jefferson said when governments fear the people there is liberty. In the same spirit, many welcome the strengthening of democracy and the increase in the checks and balances that is implicit in politicians having to take more notice of the people. The risk is that they respond by focusing on short-term popularity at the expense of long-term necessity.

How should politicians work with more empowered citizens? We'd suggest better quality communication and engagement. Holding frequent and meaningful discussions with people about important issues that affect society, and explaining why these issues matter now and in the future through a range of mediums, develops understanding on *both* sides.

In a shared power world, social media gives citizens a voice, and with it the power to shape decisions. Governments are yet to properly adjust to having a conversation.

Organized campaigns

Online campaign groups are fast, flexible and technically savvy. They mobilize citizens to form powerful issue-led lobby groups that can respond at speed to the issues of the moment. Political and business leaders can be taken by surprise by the speed and size of the lobby groups.

Although pretty much in their infancy, campaign groups are growing in influence around the world. Campaign groups – 38 degrees (UK), Move On (United States), GetUp (Australia) and Avaaz (global) – already have (early 2013) an overall membership of around 9 million people. They are growing daily.

Consumers

It's a tenet of good business that you put your customers first. In the past, businesses found out what people wanted and liked through market research. They decided when and how the research would take place and how the results would be used (or in some cases ignored). Now consumers are conducting online conversations about businesses and products and affecting each other's buying decisions.

Social media spreads bad news rapidly. When companies have a product failure the news travels rapidly among consumers.

Customers' choices about what and where they buy is influenced by the news they pick up on Facebook and Twitter. Pretty quickly, sales can drop, cash flow tightens and share prices plummet. Here is one of many examples.

Example: Yum Inc

Yum has nearly 5,300 mainly KFC restaurants in China. With a strong reputation for high-quality food, it has grown briskly in a country where there have been some serious food safety scandals. But Yum was shaken in November 2012 by revelations that two of its poultry suppliers purchased chickens contaminated with high levels of antibiotics.

Yum suffered an immediate backlash on social media across China. Yum forecast a 25 per cent drop in sales for the first full quarter following the scare. Shares dropped 14 per cent.

'One thing we've learned is news travels fast in China. This is the first time we've seen social media have a profound impact on results' (*Morning Star* analyst RJ Hottovy, Reuters News Report, 5 February 2013).

Ethical behaviour

It's no longer just about price and product design or quality of service. These matter, but the 'character of a company' matters too. Choices are being made based on company values and whether company behaviours match those values. Ethics are coming back into fashion. More people now ask whether something is ethical, irrespective of whether it is legal.

Politicians are following the trend. There was public outrage when Bob Diamond, then CEO at Barclays, resigned following the Libor fixing scandal and was recompensed with a £20m bonus. The Chairman of Barclays was called in front of a UK Parliamentary Select Committee. Bob Diamond decided to forgo the bonus.

Putting corporate tax avoidance on the agenda at the G8 summit in mid-2013 was, in part, generated by citizen outrage. People were angry because they paid their taxes even though their incomes were low or they'd had no pay rise for successive years. Then they found out that corporate giants chose to avoid paying taxes and that governments allowed it to happen.

Picking up the angry mood, politicians moved smartly into action, making tax avoidance an international priority. The politics were good – cracking down on tax avoidance was popular and likely to increase tax revenue.

Business leaders are taking a lower profile. They will lose revenue by changing tax strategies. But they will lose more money if consumers choose to take their business elsewhere. In this triangle of government, business and consumers, the consumers are more influential than governments. It's not yet clear whether consumers will vote with their credit cards for ethical business.

Doing business differently

Lord Browne and Robin Nuttall, in a McKinsey article (2013), reinforced the need for a new approach to engaging with the external environment. Citing a McKinsey survey among 3,500 executives around the world, less than 20 per cent reported having frequent success influencing government policy and the outcome of regulatory decisions. Browne and Nuttall argue:

> The success of a business depends on its relationships with the external world-regulators, potential customers and staff, activists and legislators. Decisions made at all levels of the business from the boardroom to the shop floor, affect that relationship. For the business to be successful, decision making in every division and at every level must take account of these effects. External engagement must be part and parcel of everyday business. *In our experience, most executives share that objective, but many do not know how to achieve it.*

Leaders need to build into their organization's DNA an understanding of shared power and the perspective of being part of a wider societal system. Operational decision making is messier when power is shared. Control is reduced. More people are involved. Information must be shared. Activities must be more transparent. Different views need to be taken into account. Finding solutions takes longer.

Adjusting to this change is a challenge for leaders and organizations used to operating in a sole power context.

Doing politics differently – soft power

Joseph Nye (political scientist, leading academic and former US government official) identified the concept of soft power (2006). Soft power is the ability to shape the preferences of others by attraction. Nye argues that countries influence through both hard power (threat and inducement) and soft power that creates an attraction and empathy for the country.

To give you some examples:

Hard power tools include military force, economic sanctions and intelligence services: soft power tools include cultural attractions, political values (democracy, free speech, independent media and judiciary), and the legitimacy of a country's foreign policy (compliance with international law, consistent application of principles).

Nye is clear that hard and soft power are both necessary. The skill is in choosing the correct mix of tools to fit the situation. He gives examples:

- While military force deterred the Soviet Union from further expansion during the Cold War, it was mainly the soft power elements that made people lose faith in the communist system.

- Soft power tools would not persuade al-Qaida leaders to embrace Western values but the young people in the Arab states can be reached through soft power interventions.

Countries may use hard power to dominate. One invades another. A group of countries impose economic sanctions on one country to force it to change approach.

Soft power is shared power. It's two-way. One side must create empathy and attraction to influence. The other side is persuaded or not. Within this simple framework the tools of soft power (culture, behaviour, foreign policy interventions) are complex and interrelated with other issues. But at its core, soft power is shared power.

Conclusion

As a society we face many problems. This is not new. Leaders in previous generations had different but equally daunting challenges. The post-war leadership set up international institutions to foster co-operation. The need for co-operation both remains and increases with political, economic and demographic change. The current generation of leaders must design what is needed for this time.

Business is under pressure to become part of the solution. Society holds the key. Instant communication enables people to organize and share views with an efficiency never known before. Society has the power to hold business and governments more to account for how they attend to what is important for all of us.

In this context, we return to our definition of politically intelligent leadership. It's the capacity to interact strategically in a world where government, business and wider society share power to shape the future in a global economy.

PART TWO
The PQ model

Introducing the model

03

Now we want to introduce you to the PQ model.

In Part One we explained the changing context that inspires the need for political intelligence. The PQ model is a set of skills, behaviours and processes designed for leaders and future leaders in business, government and non-profits who want to work together to deliver better outcomes – to deliver profit, growth and better lives for future generations.

You can use the PQ model for your own personal leadership development and to develop and support others leaders and potential leaders. In Part Two, we will explore the model in more detail. In Part Three, we offer suggestions on how you and your organization can develop your PQ capability.

What is it?

The model consists of five facets each of which is supported by five indicators. The facets are:

- futurity;
- power;
- empathy with purpose;
- trust;
- versatility.

The model

While each individual facet is a valuable capacity in its own right, PQ mastery is using all five facets operating in harmony. Figure 3.1 shows the model graphically.

FIGURE 3.1 PQ: the five facets

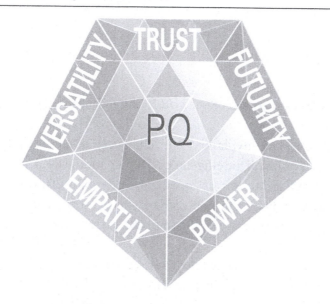

Developing the model

The idea for our model started with some work that Valerie did with Vodafone. It wanted its CEOs to be able to engage more effectively with stakeholders in their respective countries of operation. Valerie worked with Vodafone to identify the core skills required and then used these as part of an assessment process to measure the political engagement capability across the Vodafone global CEO population. We then started to wonder if this had a broader application and whether some of the principles applied to public policy leadership too.

We conducted interviews with senior leaders who had experience of working in business, government and the non-profit sector to

find out more about what was going on. What we found was consensus that government and business in particular needed to work
together more effectively and that this wasn't happening for a variety of reasons. We found that non-profit organizations have better
cross-sector relationships because many of their operations depend
on co-operation from government or support from business.

Our publishers agreed that our findings were worth exploring in
a book. Ashridge, one of the UK's top business schools, offered their
support. Armed with this, we went on to do more in-depth research
and interview leaders in the United States and the UK. We've focused
our research mainly on leaders in multinationals and international
public policy because they have first-hand experience of the challenges of working on complex projects with stakeholders from different countries and sectors. We wanted to understand what they were
doing and how they were doing it.

How the model works

The concept is that all five facets work together in harmony to create
PQ. Each facet is made up of five performance indicators.

PQ is leaders, and the indicators include a mix of behaviours, skills
and processes: in effect – what it takes to do the job. In Figure 3.2, we
define the indicators for each facet.

Descriptions of each facet and corresponding indicator follow in
Chapters 4–8. We've supplemented descriptions of the five facets
with practical advice and examples from leaders with experience of
working in shared power situations, so you can have confidence that
what we're describing works.

Harmony

When you read the following chapters, you will notice overlaps
between the facets and the indicators. The facets are all relevant to
leadership capacity. But PQ is when you use them all in harmony.
A politically intelligent leader is able to hold each facet and seamlessly move around, judging the right moment to use each one.

FIGURE 3.2 The PQ framework

FUTURITY	POWER	EMPATHY WITH PURPOSE
✓ SHAPES THE FUTURE VISION: REFLECTIVE, WELL INFORMED, THINKS HOLISTICALLY; SPOTS THE PATTERNS, MAKES CONNECTIONS WITH THE PRESENT.	✓ UNDERSTANDS WHERE POWER AND INFLUENCE RESIDE IN EACH STAKEHOLDER GROUP. BUILDS AND NURTURES RELEVANT NETWORKS AND RELATIONSHPS.	✓ STUDIES KEY STAKEHOLDERS; SEES AND FEELS THE WORLD FROM THEIR PERSPECTIVE AND DOES THINGS THAT THEY VALUE.
✓ SETS A STRATEGIC DIRECTION; IDENTIFIES PARTNERS; MOBILIZES AND ALIGNS STAKEHOLDERS.	✓ TAKES OPPORTUNITIES TO INFLUENCE AND ADVANCES THE FUTURE VISION.	✓ RELATES TO WIDER SOCIETY; CULTURALLY COMPETENT AND RESPECTFUL.
✓ REGISTERS CHANGING CURRENTS; RESETS DELIVERY TO SEIZE OPPORTUNITIES AND HANDLE RISK.	✓ ACTS COURAGEOUSLY, TAKES RISKS AND UPHOLDS ETHICS.	✓ BUILDS SHARED EMPATHY; ATTRACTS OTHERS THROUGH VALUES, BEHAVIOURS AND INNOVATION.
✓ BALANCES DIFFERENT WAYS OF THINKING: ANALYTICAL AND INNOVATIVE, STRATEGIC AND OPERATIONAL.	✓ INFLUENCES STAKEHOLDERS BY COMBINING CHARISMA AND PURPOSE.	✓ INSPIRES PASSION AND COMMITMENT FROM OTHER STAKEHOLDERS TO THE SHARED PROJECT.
✓ DELIVERS THE FUTURE VISION BY BRINGING FOCUS AND CLARITY TO COMPLEX DECISION MAKING AND DRIVING IMPLEMENTATION.	✓ UNDERSTANDS COMPLEXITY AND EXPLAINS IT SIMPLY AND MEMORABLY.	✓ FEELS EMPATHY TOWARDS HUMANITY AND ACTS TO MAKE THE WORLD A BETTER PLACE FOR FUTURE GENERATIONS.

TRUST

✓ CONSISTENTLY BEHAVES WITH INTEGRITY AND HONESTY.

✓ ACTS ETHICALLY, TRANSPARENTLY AND INCLUSIVELY.

✓ VALUES AND PUTS EFFORT INTO PROJECTS AND RELATIONSHIPS THAT DELIVER LONG-TERM AND SOCIETAL BENEFITS.

✓ MANAGES COMPETING INTERESTS WITHOUT COMPROMISING TRUST.

✓ ESTABLISHES A TRACK RECORD FOR DELIVERING RESULTS.

VERSATILITY

✓ CHANGES TACK TO FIT THE NEW DEMANDS RANGING FROM CRISIS TO EVOLUTION.

✓ EXERCISES SELF-COMMAND TO CALIBRATE RESPONSES AND PACE CHANGE TO FIT THE CIRCUMSTANCES.

✓ MAINTAINS FOCUS AND STRENGTH OF PURPOSE, BRINGS RIGOUR AND DISCIPLINE TO MEASUREMENT OF RESULTS.

✓ EXUDES CONFIDENCE; AT EASE; AND IN TOUCH WITH WHAT OTHERS NEED.

✓ RECOGNIZES POLITICAL REALITY; KNOWS WHEN TO PUSH AND WHEN TO CONCEDE; AND WORKS WITH THE POLITICS TO ACHIEVE OBJECTIVES.

Some circumstances will demand more of certain facets than others. Learning to calibrate your response in tune with the situation is part of the art of PQ leadership. You will be at your most effective when you can harmonize and move between the PQ facets effortlessly. An orchestra is a helpful analogy. Sometimes only one or two instruments are playing. At other times, every instrument is in action and in harmony. The players move in and out in rhythm with the music. So, PQ leaders move around the facets in rhythm with the demands of stakeholders and events.

Shared power

Shared power brings opportunities for innovation, diversity, scale and groundbreaking changes. It also brings complexity, competing interests, politics and misunderstanding. The challenge for leaders is how to maximize the opportunities and overcome the difficulties. We hope Part Two will support you to do this.

Futurity

04

> *Vision without action is a daydream. Action without vision is a nightmare.* (JAPANESE PROVERB)

What is it?

Futurity means being in a future state. Leaders with PQ think about posterity. Reflecting on the big issues, problems and challenges that face society, they imagine a better future where these are overcome. And, perhaps most importantly, they see how to create the conditions to make that better future happen.

Increasingly, thoughtful leaders around the world are concluding that the problems facing society and future generations are too complex to be solved by one sector alone. A partnership approach involving business, government and non-profit organizations is necessary because the power to make a difference is shared.

Is it strategic thinking?

You may be wondering if futurity is a trendy name for strategic thinking? We believe that while futurity encompasses much of the strategic thinking skill-set, it is more than the strategic thinking process. Here's why.

Strategic thinking, as you'll know, is a core competence for senior leaders. Strategy tools enable us to understand the context in which we operate, identify goals and model options to move forward from where we are now. So typical strategic thinking questions are:

- Where are we now?
- Where do we want to be?

- What is the gap?
- How will we get there?

The difference with futurity is that you start from the future and continually look back to where you are now. So unfolding events, risks and opportunities are viewed through the lens of a future state. It's what Peter Fisk (2010) calls 'future back' thinking. Futurity questions are:

- What is the desired future state?
- What is new and possible in this future state?
- What impact will changing events have on our future state?
- How do we create the future?
- What resources do we need to initiate and maintain that future?
- What demands are placed on us in the future?
- What opportunities exist in this future state?

What is futurity in a PQ context?

It is anticipating the needs of consumers, citizens and future generations, generating ideas about how to meet those needs and finding the right partners to make it happen.

The PQ context is shifting economic power, increasing populations and emerging middle classes in countries that previously have been largely poor. Global systems such as trade, finance, investment, migration, knowledge, development, the environment and security are evolving in response.

Flowing from this are major changes in demand and use of resources. Continuing to use natural resources as we do now is not practical as demand increases and resources ultimately diminish. We know this, yet governments and business in general are stuck in the present and not moving fast enough to change. Young people understand this better than most and want change. But they generally don't have the levers of power.

Leaders with PQ think about the long-term impacts on society because they are not stuck in the here and now. They're thinking about and preparing for the future. This is a key differentiator of PQ. Those who have it make time to think about tomorrow. They're conceptual thinkers who are able to:

- span time;
- make links and connections between the past, the present and the future;
- imagine what the future might look like;
- work out with others what to do in response; and
- take action.

The ability to act is critical to futurity. Leaders with Political Intelligence (PQ leaders) combine vision with pragmatism and realism, and a focus on concrete outcomes.

How do I do it?

The indicators

✓ Shapes the future: reflective, well informed, thinks holistically; spots the patterns and makes the connections with the present.

✓ Sets a strategic direction; identifies partners; mobilizes and aligns stakeholders.

✓ Registers changing currents; re-sets delivery to seize opportunities and handle risk.

✓ Balances different ways of thinking: analytical and innovative, strategic and operational.

✓ Delivers the future by bringing focus and clarity to complex decision making and driving implementation.

The indicators of effective performance in this facet are set out below. We'll unpack these indicators in the following sections by describing the behaviours and providing examples and stories to bring them to life.

Shapes the future: reflective, well informed, thinks holistically; spots the patterns and makes the connections with the present

Many of the clues to the future lie in the present and the past. PQ leaders make time to find out what is going on across the globe and to reflect on what it means for their own operations and for humanity.

Reflective

The demand on leaders at every level in organizations to have an instant response to every issue severely limits their thinking potential. With less time focused on thinking about the future, leaders are losing their confidence and capability to reflect on future challenges, innovate and create value.

Bob Zoellick, former President of the World Bank, talks about the importance of anticipation and he attributes the failure to make time for it to the 'the press of events, a full inbox, a long list of calls to return [that] can pre-empt long range thinking. People turn to immediate and usually easier tasks before facing long-term complex problems.'

Thinking time is productive time. PQ leaders make time to find out what is going on in the world, to engage with others to listen and learn, to generate and swap ideas on what is needed in the future, and by joining together to take collective action.

People reflect in different ways. The best way is the one that works for you. Some are energized by the spark of ideas and debate and are at their most conceptual and creative when sharing their thinking with others. They enjoy brainstorming, playing around with different scenarios – asking the 'what if' questions.

Others need space and quiet to 'dream' about the future and later share their more developed ideas with others as the concept takes shape.

Keeping informed

PQ leaders connect with the world differently from most people. The first thing you notice is how well informed they are about business, government, international issues and what is happening on the ground in many different places. Naturally curious, they see the world through multiple lenses and are energized by imagining the future and how to shape it.

Bob Zoellick, again: 'I read all the papers. I know what questions to ask, I prod people to think differently.' He offered the following example from his time in the World Bank. One day he noticed that world food prices were increasing. Asking his officials if this was a potential problem, he got the response that the cost of food was not a World Bank long-term strategic priority, it was a humanitarian issue. Robert, thinking in the future, could see the impact and said: 'We won't get the long-term benefits, if people don't survive the short term.'

Muhtar Kent, Chairman and CEO of The Coca-Cola Company, travels 200 days a year. He says, 'I need to see and be seen.' He places importance on keeping abreast of events worldwide. He emphasized that information comes in from everywhere: You don't know what is out there, or what is important, until you see it.

We noticed that most of the top business and government leaders we spoke to were not only very well informed, they were well connected to other influential leaders, thinkers and academics. Networking and sharing ideas is central to thinking into the future.

Committed to improving the state of the world, the World Economic Forum is an independent international organization that brings together business, political, academic and other leaders of society to shape global, regional and industry agendas. It provides an annual opportunity (at Davos) for the world's top leaders to share ideas. The participants are multinational and multi-sector. Listening to each other provides opportunities to reflect on a range of perspectives and to build relationships. It's a place for smart thinkers and smart thinking.

Future-focused and with a younger set of participants, the Annual Meeting of New Champions (the Summer Davos) in Asia is geared to innovation and finding solutions to intractable problems. Participants include young global leaders, technology pioneers, young scientists, social entrepreneurs, academics and innovators who meet and debate ideas alongside CEOs, heads of research and development, and strategy forecasters from business. Young futuristic leaders unable to attend the Annual Meeting can catch some sessions on TV.

Aspiring leaders develop conceptual and lateral thinking by learning about what is going on in the world. Exposing yourself to new thinking and different perspectives is the first step to spotting patterns and connections between events. Many of the great Silicon Valley tech companies started life with like-minded people hanging out together and sharing ideas.

It makes good sense, therefore, to invest time in gathering information and networking with as wide a group as possible. Muhtar Kent, advises young executives, to 'never eat alone'.

Thinking holistically

Future vision requires leaders to scan backwards, forwards and sideways, continually gathering data in order to understand patterns and make connections that may provide more detail about the future or identify issues that will affect it.

History

The best leaders understand history and draw on the past to bring context to today's events. Quoting Mark Twain: 'History may not repeat itself, but sometimes it rhymes,' Bob Zoellick says public policy makers should find out the history before rushing to solve the problem. Find out what worked and what didn't. Who was involved? What was the history? He poses the questions:

> How can we understand the challenges the Eurozone is facing today if we don't know the story of Germany and Europe – and the logic of integration that Europe's leaders have established as a testament of faith?
>
> How can we understand China's view of the world today and China's place in it if we don't know how China tells its own story of humiliation and revival in the modern era?

While young people have a strong sense of where we should be heading, they often lack the experience and perspective of where we have come from. Churchill (as so often) captured the sense of this: 'The farther back you can look, the further forward you are likely to see.' Too often in government we see mistakes repeated and the lessons of history ignored. Within organizations, we reinvent the wheel, trying out solutions that were tried before and failed. One of the main reasons for the frequency of this foolishness is that no one takes time to find out what happened before.

Imagining the future and what it needs leads you towards thinking about how to shape it. While shaping the future must involve innovation and an understanding of future technology, it also benefits from past experience. Basic questions are:

- What did we do in the past?
- What is different now?
- How do we bring the learning into the present?

Breadth

Holistic thinking involves looking beyond your own organization to what others can offer, finding ways to include them and seeking to create value for all stakeholders. Businesses may start out thinking their job is to deliver a new service but in a shared power world, quite soon, they find that government and society have stakes in the game. It's no longer a one-dimensional service delivery operation but a network of interrelated issues, values and dilemmas.

Google's motto is 'Do no evil'. A positive force in society, Google's search engines make information globally available and easily accessible. Google initially launched its internet service in China with censored material. Facing a barrage of criticism from users, it challenged the authorities' warnings four years later, redirecting Chinese users to its unrestricted Hong Kong site. More recently, Google was put under pressure by politicians and users to control access to child pornography through their search engines.

Google, a tech company, found that delivering a first-class search engine is not the whole job. Listening to users and handling political pressure, its leaders are defining the ethical boundaries that will shape the use of the internet in future.

Links and connections

We asked some of our interviewees to draw their approach to thinking about the future. Although many claimed this would be difficult, they had a go. All the drawings included circles and feedback loops, were complex and interconnected. Vision, strategy and delivery were shown as a non-linear, dynamic process. Scanning and making connections across a system that had many variables that potentially enhanced or blocked progress, they stayed alert to changes and took appropriate action to keep their vision on track.

Travelling widely to meet people and understand what they are doing and thinking is a great opportunity to make connections and perceive possibilities, as well as to draw people, their ideas and talents towards you.

Diversity of perspectives, ideas and experience helps develop future vision. Creativity flows from thinking differently and revisiting problems from new perspectives. Invention is often triggered by drawing on other applications and thinking about how to use them in a different context. Adding value develops out of spotting opportunities to adapt what you are doing so that with little extra cost it can be useful elsewhere. There is so much scope for business with all its entrepreneurial talent to contribute to helping society. Business leaders with vision are missing a trick if they don't take the opportunity.

Sets the strategic direction; identifies partners; mobilizes and aligns stakeholders

We cannot build our own future without helping others to build theirs.
(President Bill Clinton, State of the Union Address, 2000)

Setting strategic direction

As soon as an idea forms, leaders start to think about how to turn it into reality. In setting direction, some of the metaphors we heard used were from sailing, where the 'North Star' is perceived as the vision and the strategy the course that is charted.

Mark Sedwill, former NATO Civilian Representative in Afghanistan, explains his approach:

> You build a strategy with stepping stones, putting all the pieces together and plotting a course – a way through. Use every opportunity to move the agenda forward. Give everyone enough of what they need so that in time you build agreement. Remember diplomacy is not about talking to your friends.

Identifying partners

Achieving a future outcome that benefits many stakeholders usually needs more than one organization to do it. Finding the right partners (just like the right staff) is serious work and determines the success of your project. Partners may be single or multiple. If multiple then the web of relationships to manage is more complex.

You may not always have a choice over who you partner with. For example, a mining company like Anglo American to operate in Chile must partner with the state-owned mining company. They have no choice if they want a licence to go ahead.

Coca-Cola wants to make its operations more sustainable by developing environmentally friendly plastic bottles. It is in a position to choose a partner in the science and academic communities. (They in fact, chose a university in India.)

A non-profit organization like the Gates Foundation often needs multiple partners: sister humanitarian organizations to co-ordinate effort, governments to get a licence to operate, and business to help delivery.

During the inevitable tensions of a complex project, the quality of relationships and having a shared vision and set of values is very helpful. So how do you decide who is the best-fit partner? Here are some questions to ask about them:

- How committed are they to the overall vision?
- How aligned are their values with yours?
- How aligned is their track record with their values?
- Do they have the skills and experience needed?
- Do they have the other resources needed (finance, infrastructure, influence)?
- How are they perceived by stakeholders?
- How well do the key players on each side get on?

Mobilizes and aligns stakeholders

Why is this important? Setting the strategy includes:

- lining up stakeholders to support the project(s);
- increasing scale through sharing expertise;
- building momentum; and
- raising funds.

Here are some examples to show what this looks like in practice.

Mobilizing stakeholders – the Clinton Global Initiative

After a lifetime of attending meetings where issues were discussed and no action was taken, in September 2005, President Bill Clinton began the Clinton Global Initiative. The idea was to bring together world leaders, forward-looking CEOs and philanthropists to commit to take action on pressing global challenges.

After eight years, members have made 2,300 commitments at annual meetings that total $73.5bn. A staggering amount that, it is estimated, will improve 400 million lives.

(Extract from Clinton Foundation website.)

Mobilizing and aligning stakeholders in the World Bank

On page 51, we touched on the World Bank example. We'll expand it here as it's a great illustration of mobilizing and aligning stakeholders to deal more effectively with a complex international issue.

In 2007, world food prices surged and fuel prices soared. At the World Bank there were different views; some suggested relying on returns from high commodity prices to allow most countries to offset the danger. Others (as noted earlier) said it was a problem best handled by humanitarian agencies, rather than the Bank.

Bob Zoellick, then Head of the World Bank, set the strategic direction. He explained: 'We needed to focus on getting people through the short term to get to the long term.' The long-term future state was more farm production, more productivity and more earning power for the people.

The World Bank, for the first time, reached out to civil society groups to build support, gain information and assist partners in the field. They connected the agricultural, humanitarian food and nutrition policy communities, which often go their separate ways. International actors such as the Gates Foundation were brought in as critical partners.

Working on agricultural value-chain issues, improving financing arrangements and developing the private sector, allowed them to move towards the future state.

Mobilizing and aligning stakeholders to the cause got the job done.

'I went outside the World Bank boundary and brought in humanitarian agencies and NGOs, you have to get things done' (Bob Zoellick).

Aligning strategies with partners and relevant stakeholders enables leaders to increase scale and impact. For example a government regeneration project might include many sub-projects involving both the commercial and non-profit sectors. Each partner has its own focus: commercial sector – profit; non-profit sector – relieving inequality. But working both singly and jointly they can create a larger effect than government alone. Edmund Rose, Director of Airline Planning at Virgin Atlantic, reflects that 'airlines and governments can deliver for themselves and for wider society when there is alignment of strategic purpos'.

Inclusiveness

Building an inclusive relationship with stakeholders so that they feel empowered and able to contribute creates the conditions for alignment and a productive outcome. We'll close this section with a private sector example: how Honeywell Aerospace mobilizes and aligns its most important and powerful stakeholders – its customers.

CASE STUDY How Honeywell aligns with its core stakeholders

Honeywell Aerospace has been at the forefront of military and civilian aviation for over a century. And in the last 40 years it's also supported the space industry. Their global customer base (government, airlines, armed forces) is very powerful and demands top-quality products and services.

Honeywell is committed to technical excellence and had a long standing Customer Advisory Board (CAB) in place for over 30 years. Problems started to emerge when the company and the CAB could not agree on how to resolve in-service product issues.

Honeywell decided that it needed to connect more effectively with its customers by overhauling the way the CAB and the company interacted. It took the following actions.

- First, Honeywell asked the CAB to select a chairman from among its membership. The chairman would be the strongest bridge between Honeywell and the CAB members, facilitating resolution when progress was difficult.

- Second, it asked CAB members to represent all customers and not just its own interests, and consult on both issues and priorities for improvement.

- Third, it made CAB members 'insiders'. Each member signed a Non-Disclosure Agreement (NDA) that enabled Honeywell's engineering team to discuss every aspect of the technical investigation, the design considerations and the commercial implications of these. This action alone transformed the quality of the discussions and significantly grew the problem-solving capabilities of the CAB.

Outcomes that flowed from these actions included the creation of the 'One List', a prioritized list of actions for Honeywell. Having the 'One List' allowed the company and the CAB to speak with one voice and be figuratively and literally 'on the same page' as they focused their collective efforts on the most important issues needing resolution.

The Honeywell leadership became fully engaged with the CAB and members' voices were heard through providing electronic voting tools during the meetings.

If members disagreed, it showed on the live display, and in this way the debate continued when it was necessary to have further discussion.

'Working teams' that were composed of customers and Honeywell staff were set up to deal with technically difficult issues. In this way the customers' input was sustained throughout the problem resolution process.

The Honeywell Aerospace Advisory Board, known as the Global Customer Council (GCC), has been operating in this manner for a number of years. The results speak for themselves, with key issues being resolved quickly and effectively and the customer satisfaction scores rising constantly, most recently achieving the highest score that Honeywell has recorded.

Registers changing currents; re-sets delivery to seize opportunities and mitigate risks

No battle plan survives first contact with the enemy.

(Helmuth von Moltke)

A strategy is a map to inform implementation of a future vision. It's not a blueprint of the future. It must be refreshed, changed or adapted as necessary in response to changes in the environment.

Recognizing that adapting strategy to reflect changes in the environment is necessary reinforces the importance of a clear and well-communicated future vision. It's easy to lose sight of your intent when things are changing fast. Strategies implemented without a clear future vision will deliver something, but it may not be what anyone wants.

Complex problems overlap and so do future visions. Sometimes leaders have to choose which vision is the most important.

As we write, Western democracies debate the use of air strikes in Syria following the use of chemical weapons on the Syrian people. Some want action to send a signal to all that use of chemical weapons is intolerable. Their vision is a world where chemical weapons are not used. Taking this action shows resolve towards achieving that aim and discourages others from doing it. Missing from this evaluation is consideration of the impact of air strikes on the future of the Syrian people.

Others want to know the future vision for Syria before committing to strategic action. For them, without clarity about the future vision for Syria, the West lacks the tools to evaluate whether an air strike will help or hinder a beneficial outcome for the Syrian people.

Making decisions is tough when there are multiple stakeholders and complex problems. It requires working with more than one future vision as problems and stakeholders overlap. Ultimately, when a choice is necessary, it means prioritizing one vision ahead of another. In a shared power world that requires a high level of consensus.

Changing currents

Governments, businesses and non-profit organizations all operate in a world of constant change and low certainty. Disruptions will occur. Addressing them openly and creatively usually improves the original strategy and provides opportunities not previously envisioned. Taking a positive approach that reframes the disruption as potentially transformational turns it from a disabling force into an enabling one for all involved.

Uncomfortable and potentially threatening disruptions necessitate immediate action. While we might all feel like burying our head in the sand at times, ignoring the warning signals is dangerous and often flows from fear of derailment. In reality, positive action reduces the risk of derailment.

Think back over your own experiences. How many times has the unexpected made a project more successful? If, like us, you find the answer is surprisingly often, then the lesson is to welcome challenge and disruption and use it as a positive force.

Jeff Bewkes, Chair and CEO of Time Warner, encourages challenge in the boardroom. He says:

> We seek out conflicting visions. We need to know the assumptions that underpin decisions. Ask what is the alternative plan? And ensure we know why were not doing it. Sometimes when things go wrong it is

because people are too attached to their own issue and can't let go of it. As a leader, you have to be able to distinguish it.

Re-set

Re-sets are moments when leaders press the pause button, review a strategy and make adjustments. Usually prompted by a change in circumstances or an external event, re-set moments include changes in resources (more or less), changes in demand and changes in consumer/citizen attitudes.

Significant changes in the external environment create major re-set moments for most organizations. Major re-set moments go beyond adjustment of strategy. Creating opportunities to enhance the future vision, they are transformational. For example the introduction of mobile technology was a major re-set moment for all sectors.

Making technology faster and more accessible had and continues to offer profound opportunities for every provider of online services across industry and government and non-profits. Consumers benefit by accessing services on the move with smartphones. All users are better informed because information is immediately available and they can get things done in the moment.

Business is more efficient because it enables more real-time activity. Non-profits working with people on the ground in remote areas benefit from better communication and flow of information between sites with internet access.

Viewing disruptions as feedback offers the freedom to question and re-set the strategy. At Coca-Cola, Muhtar Kent describes re-set as a wholly positive process that keeps Coca-Cola alive, responsive and successful in a global environment.

While PQ leaders are quick to spot re-set moments, working in a joint public/private partnership does not always lend itself to rapid adjustment. Denise Holt, a former British ambassador to Spain and now a non-executive director on a number of boards including HSBC Bank Plc, notes that government and business have completely different timelines and processes for delivery. Business is generally able to make decisions quicker and then act faster. Finding ways to manage government processes, so the advantages of business fleetness is not lost, is worth addressing from the start.

Risk

Implementing strategy is messy both in government and business. Implementing strategy in a shared power world is even messier. Moving forward towards a shared vision necessitates dealing with risks.

Risk management is iterative and ongoing through the life of a project. It consists of three elements:

- anticipation and mitigation of risks;
- monitoring risks; and
- managing risks.

Designing strategies to meet future vision must involve anticipation of risk. Strategies that contain high levels of risk that cannot be mitigated are usually not viable, unless you are in an extreme situation and have no choice.

Testing the robustness of your strategy therefore includes identifying risks and finding ways to mitigate them. Some mitigation strategies might be put in place immediately. Others wait until the risk materializes. The important point is that you have the mitigation or contingency plan ready to implement should the need arise.

So, for example, a proposal to build new infrastructure might incur community opposition if the safety measures are not fully communicated. In that situation you would put a communication plan into action immediately to mitigate the risk before it occurs.

A new service might be dependent upon another project that is providing power to the community (electricity, say, or fast broadband). If the other project fails, it limits the quality of the new service. In these circumstances, you need monitoring arrangements in place and contingency plans for your project should the other project fall behind schedule.

Monitoring risk

Monitoring risk is essential. Risk registers are used widely and work when they contain meaningful information and are supported by proper monitoring systems. Too often they are bureaucratic tools that produce a piece of paper full of green traffic light signals that do not reflect the real situation but give leaders temporary peace of mind.

Complex shared power projects are often a series of projects moving towards the future vision. Projects will be co-dependent. Vital to effective monitoring is honest communication between the project leaders, and that relies on all players giving and receiving reliable data.

The financial crisis highlights the complexity of monitoring risks. Risk management is integral to trading on financial markets. Trading firms use a range of metrics to assess risk before deciding their trading strategy. Yet despite this sophisticated understanding of risk, their leaders and the financial regulators missed the big risks and disregarded those who drew attention to them.

Reliable information is essential to risk management, but so too is a cold dispassionate approach to the metrics that enables objective assessment that is not clouded by emotional attachment or greed.

Bill Gates, founder of Microsoft and now joint head of the Gates Foundation, epitomizes these qualities according to the rock star and activist Bono. In an interview with Charlie Rose on Bloomberg TV, he described Gates as being as cold and dispassionate as the dawn. He went on: 'I think I'm tough minded, but he [Gates] is tougher. When things get really serious, Bill gets more serious. He's unromantic. He wants to know what is going on' (Rose, 2013)

What is so compelling for those who want to be great leaders is the contrast between the commitment, passion and dedication Gates undoubtedly brings to his work and the versatility that allows him to switch into stark objectivity when the situation demands it.

Managing risk

Effective monitoring helps you identify when risks are emerging and allows you to activate contingency plans. But complex projects also fall foul of unanticipated risks. Significant risks have the potential to derail strategy if a way to manage them cannot be found. So these are often re-set moments. You need quick and reliable answers to the following questions:

- How likely is this risk to derail achievement of the future outcome?
- How effectively can I manage the risk?
- Have I got the resources/influence/relationships to do it?

Soft risks

Hard risks include financial overruns, lack of credit, infrastructure failure, technological problems, bad weather, conflict etc. Soft risks are the problems that may arise in stakeholder and partner relationships if they are not actively managed.

In a shared power world, projects involve multiple stakeholders and leaders are in multiple relationships. So the risk of relationship breakdown is higher and so are the consequences because of the volume and complexity of the relationships.

Mitigating soft risks involves putting the same or greater effort into managing human relationships as leaders give to managing finances and other parts of the operation. Building trust and empathy with others enables constructive and honest discussion of difficult issues. Creating a climate that draws everyone towards co-operation rather than self-interest pays dividends when competing interests emerge. We'll explore these issues in more depth in Chapters 6 and 7.

Balances different ways of thinking

Futurity requires our whole brain to be engaged: the analytic and the innovative, the strategic and the operational, and the emotional and rational. Jeff Bewkes comments: 'Problems appear analytical but most often they are emotional or relational.'

By engaging the whole-brain you approach every issue and decision from multiple perspectives, thereby increasing the odds of focusing on the right things. In this section we will explore analytic and innovative, strategic and operational thinking. Chapter 6 – Empathy with purpose – addresses emotional and rational thinking.

Preferences

Much is written about brain preferences and there are many psychometric instruments that describe the way we think and our preference for left or right-brain thinking. One well-known instrument is The Myers-Briggs Type Indicator (MBTI), which looks at four dimensions of personality, two of which are called the thinking functions. One of the dimensions is about our preference for sensing or intuition. Those with a preference for sensing have a preference for rational, logical thinking. They prefer to work with facts, details and numbers. They make their decisions based on concrete evidence. When thinking about time, their preference is for the present or preferably back in time, where they can recall former concrete experiences. This preference can be described as left-brain thinking.

Those with a preference for intuition prefer to think about ideas, possibilities and dreams. They are often described as visionary or creative. They like to scan for pattern and connections rather than facts and detail. They prefer to spend most of their time thinking about the future. This preference can also be described as right-brain thinking.

The value of psychometric instruments is that they help you to understand your natural preferences. Of course we can all do both, but generally most of us will have a preference for the way we think and this preference may be mild, moderate or strong. Understanding your own preference gives you the option to bring in others with a different preference to balance your approach.

Analytic v creative

PQ leaders appear to be able to balance left and right-brain thinking. Happy to spend time exploring possibilities, they're curious, playful and energetic, asking questions, probing and challenging the status quo. They do not see dreaming as a waste of time or non-productive. Staying open to trying new ways of doing things, they do not close down conversations that to others may seem tangential to the main debate.

Continually evaluating their products, PQ business leaders see whether they are benefiting or harming society and consider what the products, methods of delivery and organizational actions say about them as a company to consumers.

Policy making in government is an analytical process involving problem solving. Without creativity, narrow solutions that draw on past patterns of thought are more likely to emerge at the expense of reframing problems, evaluating options and making use of new technologies.

Strategic v operational

PQ leaders do strategy and detail. They range between the two. Having set the strategy, these leaders are equally comfortable to dive into the detail and ensure that the implementation is robust. Steve Jobs in Apple is said to have paid just as much attention to the design and fitting out of Apple stores as he did to designing the Mac or the I-phone. He understood that, however good his designs, the customer experience on the ground would sell the product. No surprise Apple is the world's biggest brand.

It's as though these leaders have their heads in the clouds and their feet on the ground at the same time. These are leaders with their bootlaces tied to the clouds.

Future-focused leaders agree on the importance of operationalizing the strategy to deliver the future vision.

Bob Zoellick is clear that leaders need to balance innovative/strategic thinking with analytical/operational thinking: 'There are people who can do the conceptual. People who can do the operational but you need people who can work in the operational arch where conceptual is linked to delivery options.'

Sir Kim Darroch, the UK National Security Adviser, says: 'A lot of foreign policy is about looking into the future and thinking about where we want to be in one month or one year or 10 years. But personally, I always link the future with the present. Doing the "what" without the "how" isn't a strategy, it's a wish list.'

Creating new landscapes that excite, inspire and engage others to be creative in the process and delivery is the leader's role. Jeff Bewkes notes that:

> It has to be dynamic. People come from organizational silos, you have to integrate different views and create co-operative relations with peers. Real innovation is at the margin, it is ongoing and constant. You cannot think leadership comes from the leader's office. Anyone at any level needs to affect some decisions. It's up down and sideways.

Here are some suggestions on balancing your thinking.

Balancing thinking

- Understand your own thinking preferences. Surround yourself inside and outside the organization with people who think differently.

- Imagine the future by dreaming until you can dream no more. Do not impose boundaries or limit possibilities. Generate as many alternatives for the future before deciding the future vision.

- Decide the future vision before moving on to plan the strategy.

- Ask lots of open questions: eg, 'What if?' 'What else?' 'What would x do?' 'What will success look like?' 'How will people behave and feel in the future?'

- Find out what other people and organizations do that you admire. What parts could you borrow and make your own?

- Challenge, from a position that indicates you are onside and want to stretch current ways of thinking.

- Project positivity. Bring hope and energy to your encounters with others. Encourage the lost or stuck to reframe their current position to one of possibility.

- Learn from failure as well as success. Do not be tempted to quickly paste over mistakes and miss the learning that avoids repetition of mistakes.

Delivers the future: bringing focus and clarity to complex decision making and implementation

PQ leaders believe it is their role to deliver the future. Futurity is more than imagining the future. It is equally driven by a passion to get things done – to move towards delivering the future vision with as much speed as possible. It was Winston Churchill who said: 'However beautiful the strategy you should occasionally look at the results.' Ability to conceptualize the future is an essential element of being a PQ leader but, as Churchill reflected, it's of no value if it does not translate into desired results.

Tony Blair, reflecting on governance in a speech on Development in 2011, observed: 'The tough part is not doing the right thing, or knowing what the right thing means. The tough part is actually doing it. It's the how not the what.' Capacity, combined with partnership and structured decision making, is essential, and the lessons on delivery are available around the world. 'I spent 10 years [as British Prime Minister] learning them and it is remarkable how many are applicable universally: deciding priorities; getting the right policy to achieve them; execution skills to deliver them; and tracking them, at the top, to make sure it really happens.'

Bob Zoellick reminds PQ leaders in public policy roles: 'What is really exciting about making public policy isn't evaluating and analysing and predicting. It is delivering results... Be a doer. Keep your eye on achieving results; on accomplishing things. You can make a difference.'

Bringing focus and clarity to complex decision making

A challenge for leaders is coping with the need to re-set while remaining on course to deliver the future vision.

Decisions on action to re-set should be based on a critical evaluation of the evidence. We used the phrase 'bootlaces tied to the clouds' earlier. This is where both the clouds and the bootlaces come in. At this point the leader must balance rigour and attention to detail with a strong focus on the future vision.

The first step is a rigorous assessment of the evidence for re-set, including the threats and opportunities presented. Focus on the opportunities helps to reframe the re-set moment in a positive way.

Out of this assessment should emerge a range of options for re-set. Good options require creative as well as analytical thinking. Creativity generates the ideas. Analysis is the critical evaluation of each option. Involving stakeholders as well as partners in generating and evaluating options makes it more inclusive and increases the diversity of options available to the decision makers.

Questions to ask when considering the viability of options for reset:

- deliver the future vision;
- are feasible and practical; and
- have enough stakeholder support.

Once a re-set option is agreed, it should be turned into a plan that is fully communicated to all involved. The focus switches back to implementation and making sure that every unit and individual involved knows what they must do differently and each plan is supported and understood by partners and relevant stakeholders. And that all plans are aligned to ensure coherent action.

Bob Zoellick suggests that all strategic plans should have enough 'play in the joints' to be deliverable. Building enough flexibility into plans enables those implementing them to make judgements about how best to deliver.

When a disruption is so momentous that it means changing the future vision, it is more than a re-set moment. It is time to step back and rethink the vision. Occasionally in public policy the vision does change with a change of political master. And that can prove challenging for officials who are committed to it. More often, the future vision remains the same despite the political rhetoric, and the changes are in the method of implementation.

Conclusion

PQ leaders are both visionaries and realists. They create and shape the future, stretching their own imagination and triggering the imagination of others.

Seeing the challenges facing society, PQ leaders create the conditions for tackling those problems in their own organizations and in partnership with others. Sharing their ideas and actively seeking out the ideas of others. Encouraging ruthless challenge to the future vision and the implementation strategy and working with others to turn the vision into a reality. And like Winston Churchill, who was trusted at the bleakest of times, they understand that results matter. You must deliver.

We close this chapter by introducing you to a group of influential leaders who are working in partnership to tackle societal challenges. We've used the Futurity indicators to tell you about 'The B Team' and at the same time show how Futurity indicators play out in a real life example.

CASE STUDY   Plan B for business: People, planet, profit

Sir Richard Branson, Virgin chief, and Jochen Zeitz, former Puma CEO and current director of Kering, launched the B Team in July 2013. Their mission is to deliver a Plan B that puts people and planet alongside profit.

The B Team consists of a diverse group of leaders drawn from business and politics, and from all over the world. Their commitment is to create a future where business is a driving force for societal benefit.

Here is their vision.

Imagining the future

The vision: To deliver a new way of doing business that prioritizes people and planet alongside profit.

Making connections with the present

The B Team note that there is:

a burgeoning population, more people are living in poverty than ever before and inequalities are increasing. Unemployment rates are at frightening levels. Non-profits alone cannot solve the tasks at hand, while many governments are unwilling or unable to act. While there are myriad reasons why we've arrived at this juncture, much of the blame rests with the principles and practices of business as usual.

Setting strategic direction

Branson and Zeitz have set three initial challenges:

- The future of leadership – a new kind of inclusive leadership underpinned by a moral compass.

- The future of incentives – working with partners to develop new corporate and employee incentive structures.

- The future bottom-line challenge – expand corporate accountability beyond short-term financial gains to include negative and positive contributions to the economy, environment and society.

Identifying partners

Branson and Zeitz are partnering with 14 global leaders, including major international business leaders, experienced political leaders including a former prime minister and president, and other influential figures in media and academia.

Richard Branson says: 'We're working with government agencies, the social sector and other business leaders to help get on top of the world's seemingly intractable challenges. We are keen to listen and learn and share with others.'

Mobilizing stakeholders

The B Team use traditional and social media to raise awareness of its project, appearing on US and UK TV, placing articles in newspapers around the world and conducting a live online broadcast to over 500 gatherings in more than 115 cities.

Input from stakeholders participating in these gatherings will contribute to formulation of plans for the first three challenges and to a comprehensive business plan. The general public are encouraged to submit their views on a new charter for better business through the website.

The long term

As the B Team launched, Jochen Zeitz describes its role as catalysing initiatives. Talking to the *Guardian*, he recognized the long-term commitment involved. He said: 'Some of the challenges will be significant and ultimate victory will be years away.'

Balancing analytic and creative

The B Team will work with partners to develop new corporate and employee incentive structures. Mo Ibrahim (philanthropist and former CEO of Celtel) explains:

> Positive market incentives operating in the public interest are too few and far between, and are up against a never ending expansion of perverse incentives and lobbying. We will work to create new incentives in dialogue with businesses, the social sector, and governments.

Identifying and mapping current positive and harmful subsidies is intended to educate and influence market and business behaviour to act positively.

Balancing strategic and operational

Although the B Team is an NGO, Zeitz, who is CEO, says it will be run like a business with clear actions, objectives and key performance indicators.

Focus on delivery

Pledging to 'start at home', the B Team members 'will focus on our own businesses and industries and do our utmost to meet the principles of better business'.

Focusing on execution and action, Jochen Zeitz highlighted that the B Team leaders have a formidable track record in delivery – having accomplished profit and worked in an inclusive and sustainable way in their own spheres. Going forwards, they'll add to the existing work of others as well as starting new initiatives.

See Putting People and Planet First at www.bteam.org

Power

05

Being powerful is like being a lady. If you have to tell people you are, you aren't. **(MARGARET THATCHER)**

What is it?

Power matters because it gives leaders the capacity to shape the future. We know from our own experience that power brings more freedom and choice. We can create something new, change what we're doing or stop something bad happening.

So, what is power in a PQ context? It's the ability to build relationships and influence others with the intention of shaping the future towards both profit and a better society. When power is shared, relationships are essential to the success of your project. Identifying your stakeholders is vital; understanding how much influence they exert and knowing how to engage them follows.

In a shared power world, thoughtful leaders know that, however important their job title, they don't have ultimate power. Power to shape the future is held in many hands. Stakeholders are diverse, complex and multi-dimensional. Issues and relationships are bouncing across different thought worlds.

How PQ leaders interact with others determines how much influence they exercise. In a shared power world you facilitate partnerships and engage stakeholder to deliver long-term benefits for society as well as profit, economic growth and funds to operate. PQ leaders encourage:

- modern business leaders to deliver value for shareholders and contribute to wider societal benefits;
- public policy leaders to interact strategically and inclusively with business to deliver for citizens; and

- non-profit organizations to harness the power of government and business to deliver effective outcomes.

How do I do it?

The indicators of effective performance in this facet are set out below.

The indicators

✓ Finds out where power and influence reside in each stakeholder group and builds and nurtures relevant networks and relationships.

✓ Takes opportunities to influence and advances the future vision.

✓ Acts courageously, takes risks and upholds ethics.

✓ Influences stakeholders by combining charisma and purpose.

✓ Understands complexity and explains it simply and memorably.

We'll unpack these indicators in the following sections by describing the behaviours and providing examples and stories to bring them to life.

Finds out where power and influence reside in each stakeholder group; builds and nurtures relevant networks and relationships

In a shared power world, stakeholders are critical to the success of any operation. Understanding this is vital. So is changing the way you interact with them. It's less about managing stakeholder relationships so that you get what you want. It's more about engaging with them to find mutual benefits. Why? Because stakeholders are more powerful, more broadly based and better organized.

> ### Why stakeholders matter
>
> When Rio Tinto begins a project the company expects to be in the project's location for the long haul, 100–150 years. Within this framework, there are countless ways the company touches its stakeholders and countless ways those individuals can affect a project.
>
> 'Stakeholders can have extraordinary power. Not only can they thwart progress, but they can threaten to halt a multi-billion dollar project already years underway. The success or failure of a project hinges more on stakeholder engagement than technical issues' (Judy Brown, Chief Adviser on Stakeholder Engagement for Rio Tinto).

You will notice that this indicator requires both systems and processes for gathering stakeholder information to understand the power map surrounding your project and the interpersonal skill to build and nurture relationships.

Systems and processes

The start point is effective stakeholder mapping. You need systems in place to identify the people who exercise real influence in each stakeholder group. While it is easy to pick out powerful people at the top of an organization because of their job titles, it is more difficult to identify who exercises real influence at other levels. PQ leaders need to know who can make things happen – get things done:

- Who does what?
- Who gets on well with whom?
- Who can open doors?
- Who is listened to because they are the experts or they have the ear and the confidence of key decision makers?

Preliminary research plays a large part in finding out the decision-making structure and the connecting relationships. Hugh Elliott, former Head of External Affairs at the global mining company Anglo American, says that stakeholder engagement is no longer a case of having a few business lunches. 'There is a massive fragmentation of power. Now, you need systems and processes in place to conduct research and prioritize stakeholders, particularly in areas such as civil society, communities and NGOs.' Risk is networked and difficult. Traditionally business would take a corporate social responsibility approach – for example building a well and getting a minister to cut a ribbon. Now business needs to go to the community first up and say 'what are your needs?'

Sir John Grant, notes that BG Group has changed its approach and moved beyond it: 'What matters is that governments like us; and finding community projects to support.' You might find it interesting to see in the box below how a powerful multinational approaches community stakeholders.

BG Group approach

BG's stated approach to stakeholder consultation is to be transparent, inclusive, culturally appropriate and publicly defensible, with the intention of developing broad community support for BG Group's presence. This includes information disclosure as well as more participatory forms of engagement, good faith negotiation and, where appropriate and relevant, the development of strategic partnerships. Consultation procedures involve:

- understanding established community decision-making conventions and protocols;

- hearing and addressing the needs of inadequately represented, marginalized or vulnerable groups;

- ensuring that identified communities have timely access to full, meaningful and accurate information, including information on positive and negative impacts and mitigation measures identified in the impact assessment;

- ensuring two-way engagement so that community issues and priorities are taken into account in business decision making;

- recording all formal consultation activities and outcomes, including the extent to which community viewpoints have been taken into consideration and all formal commitments and agreements.

Types of power

Multi-sector projects where power is widely shared will have both formal and informal power networks in operation. Understanding the formal power network means knowing the leadership structures and decision-making authorities and processes. Understanding the informal power networks means knowing who has influence both within and outside the organizations. When are decisions made – in the formal meetings or in pre-meetings? Who is in the room when decisions are really made?

The business and strategy author Art Kleiner (2003) identified that in many organizations there is a core group of people who influence decisions. They get their power not from their positions but because of the influence they have on decisions. The source of influence and power may vary.

One former adviser in the British Prime Minister's office tells this story about influence. 'When Tony Blair became the British Prime Minister in 1997, a number of senior government officials saw Alastair Campbell, the No 10 Press Secretary, as an official who briefed the media. Others, more quickly, recognized that he was a key source of influence on the Prime Minister.'

Sometimes those holding formal power – having the most senior job title – do not exercise as much power as people expect. Lord Green, Minister for Trade in the UK Government and former Chairman of HSBC, comments on 'how often the person at the top has no levers to pull both in the private and public sectors'. Bob Zoellick, former Head of the World Bank and US Trade Envoy, commented wryly that 'the [US] President does not have the power people think'. He drew the parallel between Obama and Lincoln. Both were re-elected for a second term but faced real challenges to get their policies implemented.

In organizations with a strong technical or legal focus, those with expert skills are the 'stars'. They hold more power because the organization relies on their expertise. No decision is made there without the experts' say-so.

PQ leaders in a shared power world are working with a range of formal and informal power structures in the other stakeholders' organizations and groups. In organizations where core groups operate, Kleiner warns that they often become self-serving; and stop making decisions in the best interests of stakeholders and society. We saw examples of this in the banking industry before the financial crisis. Some of the largest banks lost focus on their responsibility to customers, shareholders and society when making decisions on loans and trading.

Working with multiple organizations, PQ leaders need to find ways to broaden power sharing when core groups are in operation, and to introduce measures that incentivize working towards achievement of the agreed future vision rather than self-interest.

Unleashing innovation

A significant benefit of sharing power to deliver a future vision is that energy and innovation comes through new ideas and new partners. Finding partners in different sectors and countries opens up new perspectives and injects energy into businesses that might otherwise go stale. For example Procter and Gamble have opened up innovation hubs in India that work with universities and small start-ups to give them the scale to take their new ideas to market quickly (Huston and Munoz, 2013). All stakeholders benefit:

- Procter and Gamble tap into creativity and new markets.
- Small start-ups develop their businesses, create employment and contribute to economic growth.
- Students learn from the latest research, and design innovation through the universities' involvement.

Leaders, in all sectors, who work with different thought worlds (cross sector/international/cross cultural) benefit from different perspectives, innovation and new possibilities. The degree to which these opportunities are embraced varies considerably. You might like to consider the extent to which your organization engages different thought worlds.

Understanding stakeholders

Stakeholder mapping systems are essential processes to help you think broadly and systematically about who has power and influence over your activities. It's a process that helps you reflect on the identity of your stakeholders, and ask questions such as:

- How might they help you achieve your future vision?
- What risks do they pose to the success of your project?

Before moving on to discuss how to create a map, it's worth mentioning the importance of building review points into your processes. Keeping the map regularly refreshed to take account of new players, or changes in the position of existing stakeholders, maintains its usefulness. A former private secretary to a senior UK cabinet minister reinforces this point. Commenting on how government works, he observes that 'there are only a small number of people involved in every decision and they are generally senior. Business needs to know who they are and build a relationship with them. It is more complex because the senior officials change regularly.'

The map

The most basic stakeholder map should describe the stakeholder groups involved in any activity. (A stakeholder group is a cluster of stakeholders: eg, government/regulators, lobby/campaign groups, industry, competitors, customers, consumers, communities, NGOs, academia, media. The groups each contain a number of different stakeholders.) Then, summarize *what they want* (aims and objectives), and how they might *help* you.

When identifying stakeholders it's essential to think broadly across sectors. A more sophisticated stakeholder map does this and more. It identifies inter-stakeholder relationships so you can assess potential allies on an individual and group or sector level. Understanding stakeholders' spheres of influence helps you to quickly see alternative routes to engaging a wider group to support your aims.

Crucially, to be truly influential, you need to know how you can help them as well as how they might help you. Here are some core questions that leaders should be able to answer for each stakeholder group.

Core stakeholder questions

- Who are your stakeholder groups?

- Who are the stakeholders and key contacts?

- How will your planned operations affect them?

- What do you need from them to achieve your objectives?

- What do they need from you?

- How might you contribute to their community?

- How might you mitigate the adverse impact of your activity?

- Who else shares their needs/objectives?

- Who else can they influence?

- What can you do to meet their needs?

- How can you support them?

- What can you learn from them?

- How can you engage with them productively?

Once you have the core information about stakeholders, you can agree a plan for engaging them. To help you prioritize your efforts, use a grid that analyses them by levels of support and influence (see Figure 5.1).

Knowing where your stakeholders sit on this grid helps you decide how to allocate your resources. It's important to maintain and build on support, particularly with the highly influential/highly supportive groups. They have power and need to be kept on your side.

The highly influential/not supportive groups have power and are not on your side. You need to win them over if possible by devoting time and effort to understanding their needs and finding the best way to engage them.

The highly supportive/not influential groups require less effort but should be kept warm.

FIGURE 5.1 Mapping stakeholder support and influence

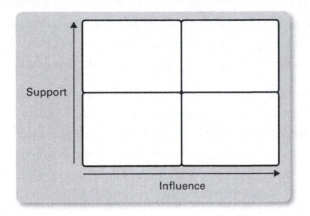

Engagement

How you engage stakeholders will vary depending upon your resources and the nature of the groups. Activities range across building a relationship with targeted individuals, setting up a forum for customers, meeting lobby groups to discuss specific issues, communicating on social media, or putting information on your website. Approaches need to be tailored to meet the needs of each stakeholder. Whichever approach is chosen, the most helpful thing is to understand why the relationship matters, both for you and your target stakeholder.

Contacts

Build into your stakeholder analysis the questions that challenge you to think beyond the obvious. Power does not just reside in the chair of the board, or the head of the regulators or the Secretary of State. It also rests with the non-executive members of the board, the official who leads on your sector in the regulatory body, the minister's diary secretary, and with the public, customers, lobby groups, suppliers, NGOs.

The challenge is to engage appropriately with all and to understand what they have to offer. Lord Jay, former Head of the British Foreign Office and British ambassador to France, advises:

> There have to be effective relationships at all levels in an organization. While you need to build senior relationships, levels vary, and you cannot look too structurally. A junior may have the best contacts and be more involved with the detail on a fairly constant basis. You need to know who the right person is and it is rarely the one you expect.

What is clear is how important it is to find the right contacts to meet our needs. Government ministries can be particularly challenging. Here is a tip from one insider: 'when targeting contacts in government remember that there are two types of government official: the first simply says "Yes" to Government ministers; while the second has the ability, expertise and confidence of the minister to be able to change their mind.'

Businesses use different approaches to finding out who has influence and power. Many large organizations have specialist public affairs departments; others employ lobbyists.

Sir John Grant shares the BG Group's approach: 'It's important to listen to stakeholders to understand their perspective and issues, and to do this BG use market research and polling companies to gather data on contacts and decision makers in some overseas countries. BG want to know who's up, who's down.'

In countries where government is closed, the media is restricted and information is harder to obtain, more support is necessary. This might be through political and risk consultancies. Smaller businesses make use of trade associations and home government support mechanisms where these exist. In more open societies, where there is transparency and widespread media reporting, it is easier to operate without external expertise. In these circumstances, research with existing contacts, the media and the internet can be sufficient.

Building and nurturing relationships

Building relationships is central to PQ power. Peter Hayes, former Head of Public Affairs at the London Stock Exchange and British High Commissioner to Sri Lanka, advises: 'build relationships with key people before you need them.'

A common mistake made by those without PQ is to wait until the moment when they or their organization want something and then

> ### Story: the 2012 Olympics
>
> Tony Blair explains how his wife, Cherie Blair, was instrumental in securing the 2012 Olympic Games for London.
>
> > Of the 120 (on the International Olympic Committee) some were the great and the good and very well known, and then you had others who worked in sports administration and they were also on the committee. People tended to make a fuss of all the big names but everyone had the same vote. My wife was very good at going to different countries and seeing the people who were the less significant people. By the time we got to Singapore, we actually knew these people, I was seeing them and talking to them.
>
> (Rajeev Syal, report in the *Guardian* on 22 July 2012, on an interview given to Sky Television by Tony Blair.)

seek to exercise influence. When power was internal and hierarchical this approach worked, particularly if you were sufficiently senior in the hierarchy. But in today's networked world it doesn't work. Power is distributed and influence *cannot be turned on overnight*.

Alexander Evans (who has worked in the US State Department for the late Richard Holbrooke and is now with the UN) recommends that leaders develop 'multiple overlapping networks, sustained over time that give you a broader contextual understanding and access to opportunities you wouldn't otherwise get'. He advises *'be useful to people and be generous'*.

Alexander makes the point about being generous with your time. Peter picks up this theme, reflecting that: 'you know that some of the people you build a relationship with are potentially important, but others you never guess will pop up in your future life. You just hit it off.'

Getting access to senior people to build a relationship is not always easy. At junior and middle levels in organizations, people are more open to meeting for coffee or lunches. These opportunities enable exchange of ideas, news and gossip. All of which incrementally build relationships. Journalists and diplomats do this all the time. Building relationships at more senior levels where access might only be possible on rare occasions is tougher. Your agenda needs to interest the senior people you're trying to meet. It helps if you have a shared contact who can introduce you. You need to know what you can tell them or do for them before you pick up the phone and get the question from their PA: 'May I ask what you want to speak to him/her about?'

Top tip

Sir Peter Westmacott, one of the outstanding diplomats of his generation and British ambassador to the United States offers some practical advice:

> When building a relationship take it out of the workplace; make it personal. You can do as much business over a game of tennis or asking someone out to a movie as you can in an office call – and they will probably enjoy it more. Make people feel welcome. Take the trouble to sit them next to or introduce them to people who they'll enjoy meeting. Friends and colleagues sometimes come to dinner and tell me afterwards, as if I'd be surprised, that they found themselves next to someone fascinating. But it doesn't happen by accident.

> Bringing people together who do not normally talk to each other and enabling them to establish a relationship is good for the British economy, good for the US economy, and good for the global economy.

Peter Hayes offers an example of getting face time with senior politicians. He invited the British Chancellor of the Exchequer to open the new London Stock Exchange. Some of his colleagues were sceptical about whether the Chancellor would accept. Peter (who knows his way around government) was able to explain the benefits to the Chancellor's office.

The Chancellor accepted the invitation. It was a win–win. The Chancellor got positive media coverage and a good photograph. The Stock Exchange got valuable face time with him.

The lesson for business is to have the confidence to ask politicians to do things and be explicit about what is in it politically for them.

Takes opportunities to influence and advances the future vision

PQ leaders focus on the future vision. Recognizing and creating opportunities to influence, they use them to advance towards their future vision. In so doing, they find allies, build support and influence those with power to make their future vision a reality.

Influence

In the past those with huge financial muscle have been able to exert unfettered influence. But things are changing. Corporate reputations have taken a hit. Lord Browne and Robin Nuttall make the point in an article for McKinsey:

> A significant minority [of people] views business executives as villains, enriching themselves at the expense of society. Even firms with the glossiest CSR reports have found themselves cast as public enemies. Take major Wall Street firms in the aftermath of the financial crisis; their relationships with the external world have been shattered and they have lost billions of dollars of value as a result.
>
> (Beyond Corporate Responsibility: Integrated External Engagement, McKinsey, March 2013)

While large companies may exercise less influence than before, it's noticeable that the influence of the general public is increasing. Campaigning on regulation, sustainability, tax avoidance and a whole raft of other issues, they have filled the void left by business's diminished reputation. They are particularly powerful in the run up to elections. Most business leaders have yet to work out how to deal with this change in the balance of influence on government.

Influencing government

Ease of access to government varies by country. Business interests are represented by national governments in international negotiations.

In the EU, members of the single market are also subject to European regulations. Access to European Commission (EC) staff and members of the European Parliament is relatively easy and this offers an opportunity for businesses across the EU to approach them directly.

Generally businesses look to national government to put their views to EC staff developing draft regulations. When you ask government to support your interests in the EU or other international forums, there are practical points about getting the timing and approach right.

Simply allowing enough time for the machinery of government to work is one factor. David Frost, International Director at the British Ministry for Business Innovation and Skills, says that when it comes to international negotiations, business underestimates the time involved to get an agreed international outcome. 'There is no clear chain of command; progress is made through consultation and consensus with other governments.' Make sure that you feed ideas in early and allow time within your planning for the negotiations to take place.

> **Top tip**
>
> Timing
>
> Business or NGOs with a need to influence government should time their intervention to have the most impact. Judging the right time relies on gathering information from contacts on how the relevant issues are progressing, who is involved and when decisions are due to be made. More junior contacts will often know this information.
>
> One senior government official advises: *'There is a window of time just before a decision is made when there is an opportunity to influence. It's vital to time your intervention to get the most impact.'*

Influencing politicians

Politicians are influenced by politics and the media. They are drawn to ideas that can be delivered within an electoral timeframe and will play well with key political stakeholders and the media. Dame

Denise Holt, non-executive director of HSBC Bank plc and former UK ambassador to Spain, comments on implementation timescales: 'Business wants a 10–15 year timeframe and ministers want a change a month. Investors work on long-term horizons; national government responds to the democratic imperative.'

It's worth remembering that key stakeholders for politicians are often inside politics rather than government: eg senior figures in their political party, influential people in their local party who select candidates for election. These are the people who the politicians rely on (with the electorate) for their jobs.

Understanding this and making your points to politicians in a way that takes full account of these facts is important. That does not mean always taking a short-term approach. But it does mean that you have to explain the political benefit of the longer-term approach and how it might be presented as a compelling case to the electorate.

Recognizing the importance of linking your request to the politician's agenda, the activist and U2 rock star Bono, talking about influencing politicians, observed: 'You stay in the room longer, if you tell them how you can help them.'

Influencing civil society/citizens

In a shared power world, it follows that government must be proactive in engaging civil society and the wider public in policy development. Forward-thinking public policy officials engage with relevant NGOs, campaign groups and academia, and share ideas and thinking on legislation. Others forge ahead, developing solutions to social problems without properly understanding the problem or seeking the views of those who are closely involved or affected by it. Often their first engagement outside their own circle is when the first published proposals attract protests.

Less often is effort put into engaging with the public on issues before deciding to act. Most politicians use social media, some to inform stakeholders, others as a way of keeping in touch with wider views. We've seen a shift towards politicians becoming more engaged with the electorate because of social media feeds. Public policy officials who are not elected seem to be more ambivalent about their relationship with citizens. They too have an opportunity to do more to communicate with the public both on developing policy and deciding on the need to act.

Influencing business

Countries with a political system that involves frequent interchange between business and government benefit from having in government people who understand business and see areas for co-operation. The US system enables a two-way flow across sectors. Yet there remains scope for more business involvement in progressing societal challenges.

Countries that have little interchange between business and government are less likely to involve business in a proper partnership because of a lack of understanding and relationships.

International development projects provide more examples of government, business and NGOs developing partnerships to tackle specific development issues such as large-scale infrastructure or energy projects.

A strategy for influencing business to become involved in a government partnership relies on understanding that business must make a profit. Proposals should include persuasive numbers on profits to encourage investment. This does not mean selling the silver. It does mean having the skills and judgement to find a proportionate balance between investment and profit.

Recognizing that business brings innovation, and a strong practical focus on delivery, should translate into involving businesses from the start in policy or service delivery design. But, rather surprisingly, business is often brought in when the strategy to deliver the future vision is already decided. Governments design the overall shape and structure of the solution before asking business to deliver it. By doing this, they miss the opportunity to engage with business to design a more innovative strategy for delivery and often create something that is not fit for purpose.

One factor influencing this is public procurement policies in countries that operate a fair and open competitive contracting process. Fearful of appearing biased towards one business, government officials are reluctant to engage business at the start because they want to maintain a level playing field when contracts are let. Public procurement chiefs face the task of redesigning procurement systems in a more imaginative way that reflects the reality of shared power.

In systems where there is no competitive process, the opportunities for working collaboratively from the start are easier to manage. The challenge in a system where there is little competition is avoiding cronyism and/or complacency.

Influencing strategies

In this section, we'll offer some ideas on what to do when straightforward persuasion won't advance your future vision.

Bubbling issues

Successful PQ leaders are ahead of the field in seeing how the game is changing and responding to it. They also have good intelligence on what pressures a regulator, minister or pressure group might be under, and know the issues that are bubbling just beneath the surface.

The bubbling issues are often fruitful areas to focus on. Most stakeholders will have issues on their radar that are not yet problems. Finding a way to avert or manage an emerging problem helps build a relationship. It delivers for them and gives you greater influence.

Everything we've said so far points to the importance of meeting stakeholders' needs to exert influence. So what do you do when you can't meet their needs? The answer is, of course, change your tactics. Here are some options.

The waiting game

The long-term game might be to wait for the environment to change (shifts in public opinion, change in economic conditions, change of government, crisis) and when the tide has turned, then, present your case. This may seem a little supine but sometimes the moment just isn't right.

Get someone else to do it

A faster approach, when time matters, is to harness the power of others to create that shift now. Going back to the points we made earlier about understanding spheres of influence – you need to find someone who can exert the influence that you can't. The following actions broaden support and can change the context:

- Forming alliances with wider stakeholder groups with shared aims and concerns, and targeting in particular those that are more influential with your target audience than you are.

- Feeding arguments through them to politicians or the media may be more influential than making a direct approach.

- Broadening support for your aims or ideas by looking for allies who would not normally be associated with your business or political interests.

Social media campaigns offer a good model. They're often made up of diverse groups with a common interest. When the British government decided to sell publicly owned forests, a broad group of campaigners coalesced, including charities, campaign groups, environmental groups, media, and a large number of citizens and voters. The government recognized the broad range of opposition and cancelled its proposals.

Here is another example on the international stage.

Example: Make Poverty History

In the run up to the 2005 G8 Summit at Gleneagles, a more unusual and powerful alliance formed between politicians and wider campaign groups. Their shared goal was to reduce poverty.

The UK government was hosting the G8 Summit and its policy objectives included cancelling Third World debt and associated interest payments to First World countries, and increasing aid to Africa. These objectives were not necessarily a priority for all G8 leaders.

In the months preceding the summit, the Make Poverty History campaign combined with the Live 8 concerts (the sequel to the Live Aid concerts of the mid-1980s) to put the issue on the front pages around the world.

International public opinion (including the Live Aid generation) and the next generation of youth got behind the campaign. They created an irresistible pressure on national leaders attending the summit to step up to the challenge and make pledges and cancel debt.

Delivering societal benefit

A core tenet of those with PQ is the belief that it makes good business sense to operate in a way that delivers societal benefit. For example, in Chapter 1 we drew your attention to Muhtar Kent's (Chairman and CEO of The Coca-Cola Company) belief that consumers are interested in the 'character of companies'. How you operate dictates your reputation. In Chapter 4, Futurity, we gave you the example of the B Team.

As ever, though, it's not quite so straightforward. The real world is messy. These leaders face challenges in balancing societal needs with their core business. Coca-Cola's core business is making sugary fizzy drinks. The obesity public health challenge is a major issue for them. And they've addressed it with new products like Coke Zero.

Sir Richard Branson's Virgin brand is criticized because many of the companies under the Virgin umbrella are not integrating sustainability into their operations. Virgin knows this has to change. Their response is to produce a new sustainability vision and strategy to focus senior managers' attention on their social and environmental impacts.

So how does Coca-Cola maintain its reputation with its stakeholders? It takes its responsibility to the community seriously. It doesn't back off from sensitive political issues when mixing business and societal responsibility. Muhtar worked with Tony Blair (head of the Quartet, overseeing efforts to sponsor peace in the Middle East) to improve the economic conditions in Palestine. Coca-Cola's business objective – it has three bottling factories in Gaza; peace and prosperity will improve its trade. The societal point – securing peace in the region would benefit society locally, regionally and globally.

In India, it works to strengthen the role of women in business to help build sustainable communities. Muhtar Kent explains that delivering societal benefit is consistent with delivering hard business value because:

- Women are reliable distributors.
- They routinely manage businesses better than men.
- They tend to build sustainable communities into which we sell our products.

Involving business in delivering for society brings the financial discipline of business. The following short case study is an example of how a social enterprise combines innovation and societal benefits in a business relationship.

CASE STUDY Portaloos

According to the UN, by 2030 20 per cent of the world's population will live in slums.

Social enterprises like Sanergy, which has 250 'portaloos' placed around one of the Nairobi slums, is leading the way in providing commercially sustainable sanitation services. 10,000 people a day are paying to use the service, which comes with free water and soap.

Sanergy sells the toilets to residents of the area, who charge around four Kenyan shillings per visit. Sanergy collects the waste each day and turns it into organic fertilizer that is sold to farmers outside Nairobi.

Acts courageously, takes risks and upholds ethics

Working in a shared power world to secure a future vision is not easy. You face multiple issues: different stakeholder interests, competing visions and mutual dependency. It takes courage and an appetite for risk. But these characteristics must sit within an ethical framework. Otherwise they tip into recklessness and disrespect for others.

Ethics

Ethics shape how leaders should behave in terms of rights and responsibilities and fairness to society. Strong ethics and values offer a solid basis for attracting others to work with you.

Jeff Bewkes, Chair and CEO of Time Warner, confirms that ethics is at the heart of leadership. He says if you have ethics, issues like transparency, rights and responsibilities all fall into place. Jeff drew our attention to an example in the political world. He highlighted the work done by the outgoing Bush administration and the incoming Obama administration following the 2008 financial crisis.

Faced with the worst economic crisis since 1929, the Bush and Obama teams worked together to fix the problem faster. President Bush, a Republican, had to approve nationalizing banks – unthinkable for his voters. President Obama, as one of his first presidential acts had to do the last thing he wanted or indeed his supporters expected. He bailed out Wall Street bankers with public money.

Both men moved beyond partisan interests and acted in accordance with their responsibilities to do the best for US citizens and for the benefit of the global economy. It was a policy success and helped the United States and Europe to avoid a much deeper recession.

In a shared power world, PQ is creating partnerships where business and society benefit. But the clear message is that behaving ethically does not mean that business operates as a charity. Business is business. But good business doesn't ignore the needs of society.

Mubadala Development Company is a $55 billion strategic investment and development company whose sole shareholder is the government of Abu Dhabi. McKinsey interviewed their COO, Waleed Al Mokarrab Al Muhairi, and asked him how his company trades off financial returns against strategic contributions to society.

Al Muhairi responded:

> We tend not to compromise on this. Part of the thinking is that if you start making those trade-offs, you'll end up on a slippery slope that can take you places you wouldn't ideally want to be. So we always use financial returns as the first filter when making an investment. If it passes the financial test, we look at the strategic metrics and see if, together, the financial and strategic metrics create a cluster or businesses that make sense from an Abu Dhabi perspective.
>
> If our shareholder asks us to do something that makes sense only from a social perspective, we'll try to turn it around and engineer it in a manner that respects the mandate of Mubadala to produce economic returns. If that doesn't work, we'll go back to our shareholder and say,

'We don't believe this is the right project from Mubadala's perspective.'
And the government of Abu Dhabi and our board of directors are quite
adamant about staying true to both sides of our mandate.

(Zafer Achi, *McKinsey Quarterly*, September 2010)

Courage

The best leaders are courageous. They have to be. However inspiring
your future vision or laudable your project, you will face criticism
from vested interests who will aim to stop activity that threatens them.

These vested interests have different levels of power to influence
others. Those with a media voice or whose views are championed by
the media have access to a ready-made audience to put their views.
Others have a more subtle influence on key stakeholders.

Opening up new ways of working, challenging the status quo and
finding new partners to replace existing ones involve significant change
and risk of failure in the early stages. Leaders champion new approaches
and carry the risk. They don't keep their heads below the parapet. You
have to be ready to take risk and sustain criticism in all sectors, often
unfairly, if you are to make a tangible difference in any sector.

Appetite for risk

An appetite for, and an attraction to, risk is a hallmark of leaders
with vision and a drive to achieve results for their businesses and
countries. Challenging future visions cannot be achieved by taking
a cautious approach. Taking risks is part of a leader's job. Having
an appetite for risk taking is a PQ leadership trait. Implementing an
ambitious future vision exposes a leader to failure. The best leaders enjoy the frisson of risk without becoming reckless. Just as fear
is perceptible, so is the self-belief that is inspired by successful risk
taking. Partners and stakeholders pick up on the leaders' confidence
and have faith that collectively they can deliver a successful outcome.

Here are a few quotes to give you a flavour of what we mean:

- Muhtar Kent cites courage as a leadership trait noting that
  'where there is no risk, there is no reward'.

- Sheikh Mohammed Al Maktoum, the visionary ruling leader of Dubai who has overseen the transformation of the UAE into an international business centre and Middle East hub, remarked 'that the greatest risk of all is to take no risk'.

- Mark Sedwill, former NATO Civilian Representative in Afghanistan and head of the UK Home Office, concludes that 'it's more than being willing to take risks, you have to enjoy it'.

- One of Sir Richard Branson's favourite quotes is nothing ventured, nothing gained – 'life is more fun if you venture' (Regan and Branson, 2013).

What type of risks do we mean?

In business, leaders who want to make a profit in a way that protects or benefits society are likely to run into challenges from investors and shareholders, because the changes may increase costs and prices and threaten short-term profits. Taking risks by changing the way their company operates, the leaders know that they must make a profit or they won't last long.

The members of the B Team (introduced in Chapter 4) recognize they must put their own house in order before encouraging others to put profit, people and planet first. By setting aspirational ethical standards for others, they run the risk of becoming targets for critics who feel threatened and therefore want to devalue the collective work of the team and the ideal.

In government, it is the public policy official who 'speaks truth to power': for example, describing explicitly to their political masters the unintended consequences of implementing an unwise policy. Or it is the politician who champions action that is not widely popular because it is in the best interests of society (eg a health measure such as smoking bans in bars/restaurants) or equality measures (eg enabling gay couples to marry).

In the non-profit world, it is the NGO that refuses to bow to political pressure or refuses a large donation from an unethical business even when funding is tight. It is the UN Mission that intercedes with dictators when regional powers and others are looking the other way.

Across all sectors, it is individuals who put themselves on the line – doing something that is necessary, but that others fear doing, to move towards achieving a better future.

So what?

We have purposefully drawn on examples from large corporations and well-known leaders in this book because they're credible and have a track record. But PQ is for leaders across sectors and countries. The challenge for all of us who want to develop political intelligence and deliver more by working with others is to step up to the mark in our own worlds. Jeff Raikes of the Gates Foundation is one of those who see the necessity of scaling up; he urges 'leaders at all levels to be more courageous in their organizations and communications by partnering with others who have shared values'.

We see at all levels in society that people are suspicious of opening up to new ideas and new people. We worry about losing control, being exploited, losing our identity. Our human caution is at odds with globalization and a more integrated world. The leaders who will make a difference for their own organizations and for wider communities are those with the courage to open up and work with others. This isn't comfortable; organizations don't change easily. Leaders need to use the full PQ skill-set to help people see the value of doing things differently.

Courage is an element of enduring leadership. Leadership that makes a difference is not about the short-term win. It's about investing in the long term and doing things that matter and offer real benefits. Risks are easier to take if you rather enjoy the challenge.

Influences stakeholders by combining charisma and purpose

A charismatic individual without a purpose is an entertainer or a courtier. Charisma combined with a strong purpose is a powerful combination that inspires and influences others.

Charisma

Joseph Nye (*Harvard Business Review*, October 2006) identified three elements to charisma. They are:

- vision;
- confidence; and
- communication skills.

Nye then added emotional intelligence to those above to describe an inspirational style of leadership.

Charisma is one of those words that can make anyone of us feel powerless. We imagine John F Kennedy, Martin Luther King, Nelson Mandela and Gandhi. Then, having set the bar so high, we become very aware of our own limitations. To inspire and influence through personal charisma requires you to demonstrate the four elements identified by Nye. Thinking about charisma as a series of building blocks makes it more attainable than trying to become JFK!

Vision

To be more charismatic, you must describe your future vision and how to make it happen in a way that captures the imagination of others. Most people are drawn to new ideas by a mix of emotion and logic. You attract others when you offer a compelling vision that excites and inspires. Even more powerful is when you move on to show how your vision is feasible and practical to implement.

Describing your future vision in a compelling way is dependent on having clarity about the future vision, why it matters and the strategy for delivery. Jeff Bewkes puts it succinctly: 'You're not likely to be influential if you're not working in a strategic context.'

Emotional intelligence

Speaking with passion and conviction makes you persuasive. When you combine this with listening to others and making them feel that their views and needs are equally important, you are more charismatic. Charisma draws on emotional intelligence, because a charismatic leader balances passion and enthusiasm, with listening and valuing others.

Confidence

Confidence breeds confidence. If you are confident, then others have confidence in you. A close aide to a senior British cabinet minister who has observed many interactions with his boss offers the following advice: 'Clarity of thought and ability to signpost clearly what you want; and the courage and confidence to believe that you have an equal right to be in the room. Ministers might be frustrated by thoughtful challenge but they will dismiss someone who seems irrelevant.'

As we've said earlier, a hallmark of leaders with PQ is how well informed they are. They are curious and they understand the world and are knowledgeable about international affairs as well as domestic issues. They draw on history to add context and many are connected to academia in some form. Most have multi-cultural experience and as a consequence have networks around the world. People want to hear what they have to say because they know they'll learn something.

Building confidence in the room also means that you have to know what you are talking about. Talking in broad terms is not enough. Knowledge and ability to bring the facts to bear are essential. Lord Kerr, then Deputy Chairman of Shell, now Deputy Chairman of Scottish Power and a former British ambassador to the United States and the European Union, comments: 'Don't be outflanked on knowledge.' If it is a technical subject and you are not expert in the detail then bring a technical expert with you.

Lord Jay reflects:

> Government ministers like people who have natural authority, know what they are talking about, are calm and thoughtful, deliver knowledge and understanding of issues in a sensible way and are not frightened of them. You need to know your stuff and how you can make a difference.

When those you seek to influence have confidence in you and want to hear what you have to say, it builds your confidence and suddenly everything flows. When you feel that flow, you have the capacity to inspire others.

Purposeful

Charisma draws people towards your future vision. Purposefulness shows you mean business and attracts those with a similar determination. Purposeful leaders prioritize achieving the future vision.

In a shared power world, you negotiate frequently with a range of stakeholders. Leaders who leave their ego outside the room and do what it takes to move the situation forward are more likely to advance their future vision.

Lord Kerr has extensive experience of negotiation, both in the boardroom and in multilateral diplomacy. He offers this wisdom:

> Negotiating success is to win the battle with no blood. The other guy is not defeated. Win the battle with no blood on the carpet and the other guy does not feel defeated. You show how you would be supportive to their needs.

Collectively, politicians and government officials can appear to other stakeholders as self-important. Having observed senior government officials who need co-operation from industry, Peter Hayes advises them to be careful of conveying a view that 'you might make money, but we run the country', which is not helpful to co-operation. This view is echoed by a senior government official who notes that: 'Government always thinks it's much more legitimate than others. It tends to consult when convenient.'

Complex projects, multiple stakeholders, changing environments mean that despite best efforts things will go wrong. Jeff Raikes of the Gates Foundation tells his staff: 'We aspire to help solve some of the world's toughest problems. To succeed, we need to take risks, and the potential for failure is inherent in risk taking.'

Stakeholders

Purposeful leaders learn the lessons and adjust activity in response to failures. However, in a shared power world with multiple stakeholders who are all connected through social media, news travels fast, and quietly adjusting your processes is not enough to reassure stakeholders. It's at these moments that you draw on the personal capital that you've built with stakeholders to maintain their trust.

Mark Sedwill, cautions: 'remember power depends on whether you are winning the argument. It ebbs and flows.' In a shared power world, 'your power is the power that everyone grants you. Don't overplay it. You only have the power allowed by others.'

Understands complexity and explains it simply and memorably

Communicating regularly and persuasively with the stakeholders is a key part of a PQ leader's role. Without stakeholders' participation, interest and support for projects, it's difficult for leaders to move projects forwards. The leaders we spoke to recognize their role as makers of meaning. They know that they need to use different channels of communication to capture a broad range of stakeholders. Involving people in their thinking, seeking their views and keeping them informed of progress and achievements builds commitment.

Persuasive communication that is meaningful and captures the interest and energy of the audience is central to influence. David Frost summarizes it well. 'The key skill is the ability to manage complexity, understand it and then to communicate it simply, with a memorable vision that motivates people.' Easy to say and hard to do!

Think complexity, speak simplicity

Communicating simply and memorably requires effort and discipline. It's a mark of respect for the listener or reader when you make an effort to do so. Clarity is gained by structuring the message to present information coherently. Alan Barnard and Chris Parker (2012), experts in public campaigning, emphasize that 'the order in which we deliver information determines the response of the audience'.

You need to be clear about what you want to say, then refine it through reworking until it is sharp and lucid. Test it out on others, get their feedback and then rework again until your messages, whether spoken or written, will be understood by your audience.

Use logic and emotion

It's an art to fully master the complexity and detail of a subject and then strip it down to the headline issues and re-present it to an audience. Those who do it well balance the right amount of detail and context with the facts so that people can understand and process the information offered. They also explain why the issue matters and where the audience should focus their attention. A focused and logic-driven approach works best with an audience that wants to know the facts.

Most people do want to know the facts, particularly in an age when government and business are viewed sceptically. People are increasingly suspicious of hype and turned off by sterile corporate communication, and by politicians and policy makers who dress up bad news behind a blizzard of facts.

Engaging your audience, however, requires more than presenting factual information. Touching people's emotions increases impact and memorability. Finding a balance between offering factual information and then putting it into context by explaining how it impacts their lives or their children's lives makes your communication more meaningful. The media understands this very well and most news stories combine both elements.

Strategic narrative

In a shared power world, just as strategy and activities must be aligned to the future vision to maintain coherence and focus, so communications must be similarly aligned. Complex projects with multiple stakeholders, aiming to deliver a range of benefits from profits through to long-term societal benefits, have to explain what they are doing and why it matters to a range of audiences.

A strategic narrative links the future vision and why it matters to all project communication. With projects that involve multiple partners this approach avoids the risk of different messaging causing confusion among stakeholders. Similarly multiple projects all working towards an overall future vision benefit from linking up the communications from each project to an overall narrative to ensure coherence.

Identifying the most important messages, then putting a process in place to ensure that all communications align to one or more of these messages, helps the various audiences understand what the project is about, why it matters and how activities relate to it.

The importance of frequent and coherent communication is particularly important when explaining changes that bring long-term benefits but have short-term disadvantages. People need to understand why it matters and what will be different in future as they face the immediate inconvenience or difficulty.

Storytelling

Stories fit into strategic narratives when they explain how the future vision will affect people's lives. Leaders turn to storytelling when they want to evoke an emotional response, or paint a picture of the future that is attractive and compelling. The skill is to stimulate the audience to imagine what they might want and understand how together they might achieve it in the future. Martin Luther King's 'I have a dream' speech is an outstanding example.

Story is one of the simplest formats to get people's attention and understanding. Stories have the power to cross cultures, generations and time; there is a story for every situation. Human beings have been programmed for centuries to tell, listen to and recall stories, it is in our DNA. For leaders working with multiple stakeholders; the ability to communicate facts clearly and simply and add colour through story and metaphor gives them the power to influence and even transform opinions.

Every skilled politician is looking for a story to tell the public that fits their political strategic narrative. Politically intelligent business leaders recognize this and respond to it by becoming part of the story and linking their business needs to the strategic narrative – eg cutting carbon emissions, increasing employment, supporting equality. As customers become increasingly discerning about what and who they buy from, the 'character of the company' and the stories an organization tells itself and others about how it contributes to wider society become increasingly important.

Story: Vodafone – telling stories

Vodafone, a young and yet highly successful international company, has traditionally developed its global CEO network from people with a background in finance or commercial functions. The early successes of Vodafone were based on the ingenuity and hard work of these engineers. As the telecoms market has become increasingly more sophisticated, it was clear that such professional excellence alone was not enough to enable these CEOs to engage effectively with their customers and government.

Vodafone's early history of being set up above an Indian restaurant in Newbury, and their ambition, was largely unknown. Yet, it has the capacity to surprise and delight listeners with its humble beginnings, coupled with ambition and belief as it became a global success story.

Similarly the colourful stories told by individuals working in new cultures and their amazing responsiveness to client needs – such as designing handsets with larger and simpler buttons for the elderly, technology to enable farmers in Africa to transfer money and not have to walk miles to market, and support systems for people with diabetes – were rarely shared.

It was clear that Vodafone needed to tell these stories, as not only are they great stories but they also tell people about Vodafone's values and behaviours. In 2011 Vodafone invited everyone in the company to submit their stories and created the Vodafone story book: a book that is a celebration of its history, staff and customers. Now when country CEOs meet people, they think about the stories they will tell, as well as the products and services they provide.

One country CEO called to say: 'I thought I would try telling a story at my next meeting with a minister. It worked, he loved it and I cannot believe that he now gets what we are about.'

Stephen Denning in *The Leader's Guide to Storytelling* (2011) suggests that narrative can be specifically used to create shared visions and to ignite action and implement change. Linking genuinely felt values to people's own lives and experiences enables us to make a powerful connection. Here is an example from a master orator.

Story: Master Orator

President Obama in his 2012 election-night acceptance speech
used narrative to share his vision of America. He talked about
responsibilities as well as rights and told a campaign story in
support of healthcare reform.

> I have seen this spirit at work in America... I saw it just the other day
> in Mentor, Ohio, where a father told the story of his eight-year-old
> daughter whose long battle with leukaemia nearly cost their family
> everything had it not been for healthcare reform passing just a few
> months before the insurance company was about to stop paying for
> her care. I had an opportunity to not just talk to the father but meet
> this incredible daughter of his. And when he spoke to the crowd,
> listening to that father's story, every parent in that room had tears in
> their eyes because we knew that little girl could be our own.

Conclusion

> The test of leaders – whether of people or countries – is how they
> deploy power, within the constraints of their time, to shape the future.
>
> (Bob Zoellick)

Leaders cannot operate in a shared power world from the sole perspective of their personal power in organization or business. Their
power is granted by others. Shaping the future when power is shared
relies on building meaningful relationships with key stakeholders.

However powerful the organization, PQ leaders understand that
they are part of a wider and connected world. They know who matters, even if they are not in the most obviously powerful positions,
and they're ready to listen and learn from them. They also realize that
they need systems and processes to ensure that all stakeholders are
included. They're willing to concede when others do and to ensure
that everyone has a good story to tell.

They've got the courage and conviction to do what is necessary
and important, and the personal presence and grit to see it through
and bring others with them. They relish risk without being reckless.

They are well informed and ahead of the game. They're generous in the time they give others and do things that are helpful to them. They have strong overlapping networks. When they need to challenge or influence, they have the credibility to succeed. They know how to tell a story so people understand why it matters. They make things happen that benefit their organization and wider society and they ensure that both needs are met.

Here is a real life case study that captures many aspects of politically intelligent use of power.

CASE STUDY   Anglo American's Quellaveco
project in Peru

Hugh Elliot, former Head of Government Relations at Anglo American, tells the story:

About mining in Peru

For Peru mining has long been both lifeblood and controversy: one of the world's most richly endowed countries for minerals has seen mining conflicts dating back to the Spanish conquest.

Anglo American has two large, undeveloped copper mining concessions in Peru. In 2010, I was despatched to the Quellaveco project in the Moquegua region to help address controversies that had brought major demonstrations out on the streets against our project.

About Moquegua

Moquegua, famous for its fruits, olives and above all its Pisco, lies in the very south of Peru, less than a three-hour drive from the Chilean border. The region knows mining; the Cuajone mine and Ilo smelter and refinery have operated for close to 50 years and controversy has dogged the industry for decades.

It was into this environment that Anglo American invested in Peru in 1992, winning an open tender for the Quellaveco deposit, which at 3,500 metres above sea level lies some 40 km and 2,000 metres in altitude upstream from the departmental capital of Moquegua. After a number of false starts, in the late

2000s the company set about finalizing its feasibility studies, mine planning and permitting.

The challenges

We always understood that water was the key issue: mines need large quantities of water to operate and Moquegua is a water-stressed area. The landscapes are vast and brown, an attenuated extension of the Atacama desert. Intermittent river valleys snake down from the high Andes, 5,000 metres and more, towards the Pacific Ocean – arteries of life that water and feed local populations. These rivers can produce torrential floods in the wet season but many reduce to streams in the dry period. Large areas of dry land are potentially fertile, so there is intense competition for water.

We had already adapted our water supply plans to avoid using groundwater, in response to community concerns. We had developed strong links with a wide range of local stakeholders through a multi-year programme of outreach, engagement and community development programmes – in themselves unusual and progressive for a project at such an early stage of development.

So we were surprised when in August 2010 more than 1,000 citizens demonstrated outside our offices after the central government had granted us a key water licence. The government suspended the controversial licence in the following weeks. As we had been preparing for the imminent development of the project, we had underestimated just how much local people were concerned about what lay ahead.

Instead of pressing our case with the authorities – the classical industry response – our chief executive flew to Peru to meet regional president-elect Martin Vizcarra, who was to play an important leadership role in the negotiations that followed. We agreed, to press the pause button on the project and participate in a multi-stakeholder dialogue process – known as the 'dialogue table' – to address and seek to resolve local concerns. These focused on water, our environmental impact and the company's social contribution to the region.

Our response

I arrived in Peru to help direct our approach as these unprecedented negotiations took shape. The auguries were not auspicious. Dialogue tables in Peru have a history of being long-drawn-out talking shops that end in disagreement. But together with our Peruvian colleagues in Lima and Moquegua, we took a number of measures that proved to be critical to success.

First, we engaged with our stakeholders to ensure that we had a comprehensive understanding of their interests. There were more than 30 civil society, professional, governmental and industry associations that made up the Quellaveco Dialogue Table, and many more groups took an active interest from outside.

Second, we adopted a more transparent approach, ensuring that our plans – and crucially how we planned to ensure that water quality and quantity would not be negatively affected by our project – were properly understood. We ran dozens of visits to our prospective mine site, established information centres in all the main population centres, extended our community outreach and generally delivered what was probably the most open, transparent and widely communicated programme in the industry.

Third, we engaged directly with the members of the dialogue table – whatever their views about our project. Quellaveco had its supporters, but many were doubtful and some downright opposed. We were ready to talk to everybody. At the dialogue table we presented our plans, subjected them to independent scrutiny, listened to concerns and, crucially, responded to these.

After 18 months of detailed negotiations, the dialogue table was successfully concluded in August 2012, with Anglo American making an important series of commitments including:

- major additional infrastructure works, in partnership with the local government, to deliver a significant increase in water availability for agriculture, helping address the seasonal and annual fluctuations in rainfall;

- major changes to the mine closure plan to restore the river valley to its original course;

- a broad programme to promote local content to help the project deliver more benefits for the region and for Peru – local employment guarantees, including 80 per cent of locals in unskilled jobs, local training to upskill workers, supplier and enterprise development initiatives, and the establishment of a local development fund;

- environmental programmes to better understand and protect local wetlands, fauna and flora;

- joint monitoring, with civil society and local government representatives, of compliance with our commitments.

Our experience

The most important feature of the dialogue table, however, was the readiness of almost all participants to take the time to listen to the concerns of others, and as a result a much deeper understanding ensued. Whatever their individual opinions about the project – and though the large majority are now in favour, support is by no means universal – local communities now appreciate the transformational opportunities that such a major investment offers for their own development. They understand how risks can be effectively managed in a modern mining operation. And in Anglo American, we have a profound understanding of community interests and concerns and we are much better placed to respond.

The dialogue was difficult at times. The loss of control it implied was uncomfortable, to say the least. Corporations generally prefer control. But the reality is that, in the networked world, power is increasingly fragmented and business success will depend on understanding and addressing all centres of power, formal and informal.

This is a positive start for Quellaveco and a unique experience for a mining project in Peru. All stakeholders played an important part. As well as the regional government, the Humala administration deserves credit, too. They invested in the process and stuck with it through its ups and downs, demonstrating that it is possible to envisage a different model for mining, where conflict is replaced by collaboration.

At Anglo American, we are proud of the positive difference we are making, and I learned greatly from my work on the ground during the process. But equally, we are conscious that the dialogue table is just the start: there is no doubt that there will be bumps along the road as we develop such a major project. A robust implementation of our commitments and ongoing, open dialogue with our stakeholders will be critical to success.

(Article published in the *Guardian*, 12 April 2013).

Empathy with purpose

06

"*No one cares how much you know, until they know how much you care.* (THEODORE ROOSEVELT)

What is it?

Empathy is the capacity to imagine oneself as another person, emotionally to feel what the other person feels, cognitively to know how the other person sees the world.

Empathy with purpose in a shared power world means building strong and trusting relationships with stakeholders who are central to the success of a shared project, and using the shared relationship to achieve outcomes that offer mutual and wider benefits.

Is it manipulative?

> The ability to read people is an art. The humanness of it all. It takes time and investment – but it can be the key to the door.
>
> (Judith MacGregor, British High Commissioner, South Africa)

You may think that having a purpose or finding 'the key to the door' is manipulative behaviour. It could be. But, it does not have to be. Empathy with purpose is positively intended. The driver is to connect with people at the level of emotion and values, to find the shared beliefs and to work closely with them to deliver long-term solutions that offer a range of benefits.

How does empathy with purpose work?

PQ leaders can literally feel their way into understanding and relating to others. This requires reflection and the mental and behavioural agility to temporarily move from their inner world to occupy another's. Gaining these insights helps build rapport at speed, see the situation from multiple perspectives and suggest ways forward that meet the needs of multiple stakeholders.

The ability to imagine oneself as another person is not easy. Even when we stop to think about others, we tend to imagine their reality from our own perspective. If we lead only from our own perspective we are in danger of making false assumptions about how others are experiencing the world, what they want, their motivation, beliefs and values. This lack of insight significantly reduces our capacity to work in partnership.

Who are the natural empathizers?

Research suggests that the natural empathizers are top business performers, women more than men, and alpha male chimps!

EQ tests suggest that women are generally more empathetic than men. For example, in 2003, an article in *Neuroreport* (Simon-Thomas, E, 2007) reported on how men and women responded when they were asked to identify others' emotions. Women's brain activity indicated they were truly feeling the emotions they saw, whereas the men's brain activity indicated they were rationalizing what they were feeling.

While this may be true across the whole population, we've found that *a hallmark of male PQ leaders is their ability to empathize and connect with others.*

Ruth Malloy, a psychologist, at Hays Group, Boston, studies excellence in leaders. When she looked at the top 10 per cent of business performers she found no gender difference in emotional intelligence. When Valerie worked with Vodafone to review the political engagement capability of their country CEOs, they found that the highest performers also had the highest empathy scores. Both experiences suggest that the best leaders have empathy regardless of gender.

Daniel Goleman, the author and thought leader on *Emotional Intelligence*, in an article in *Psychology Today* (2011) drew readers' attention to a study of primates. The study found that while female chimps give solace to another upset chimp more often than male chimps, the alpha male chimps give solace even more than the females.

So how does empathy with purpose work in a PQ context?

We believe empathy with purpose works at four levels, starting with an ability to empathize with other people and moving beyond to empathize more broadly across organizations and with humanity. Let's explain:

- Developing empathy in relationship with individuals: the ability to listen, understand and develop a deeper relationship that in the longer term may increase your capacity to influence partners and stakeholders.

- Creating empathy among others by doing things that attracts them to connect with your organization or country.

- Building and maintaining empathy amongst those engaged in delivering a shared project as partners or stakeholders.

- Having an empathy with humanity: PQ leaders feel a responsibility to others and want to leave a positive legacy for future generations.

How do I do it?

The indicators of effective performance in this facet are set out below. We'll unpack these indicators in the following sections by describing the behaviours and providing examples and stories to bring them to life.

The indicators

- ✓ Studies key stakeholders; sees and feels the world from their perspective and does things that they value.

- ✓ Relates to wider society; culturally competent and respectful.

- ✓ Builds shared empathy; attracts others through values, behaviours and innovation.

✓ Inspires shared empathy and commitment from other stakeholders to the project.

✓ Feels empathy towards humanity and acts to make the world a better place for future generations.

Studies key stakeholders: sees and feels the world from their perspective and does things that they value

Studying stakeholders

Empathy with purpose works at both a personal and organizational level in a PQ context. You need to know how key stakeholders and their organizations perceive the world, and from this determine how you and your organization need to behave to achieve progress.

PQ leaders have a two-pronged approach to stakeholder management. First as we described in Chapter 5, Power, they take a systematic process approach to stakeholder identification and means of engagement.

Second, and this is what differentiates them, is that they believe it's important and therefore invest time in both emotional and cognitive empathy to understand how other people and organizations see the world and what they want.

Knowing the other person's history and preferences, combined with empathy, oils the wheels of a relationship, enabling it to move at speed because you understand each other and can best guess how each other will respond.

Example: The ambassador (I)

Before presenting his credentials to President Clinton as British ambassador to the United States, (the then) Sir John Kerr made time to attend seven events where he knew the President would be speaking.

Sitting close to the front, he was able to supplement what he had already read about the President with his own direct observations.

The additional benefit of his research was being seen by President Clinton in the audience showing an interest.

Lord Kerr's advice is: 'Study the person as well as the file. Warm up the person by doing things that are important to them.'

Making a connection is easier when you know something about what matters to someone, such as their interests and experience. A female non-executive director recounted a story of sitting next to the chairman of a global bank for the first time at a dinner. She recalls it was a good conversation. Little of it about business, mainly they talked about rugby. Although not a fan of the sport, she sustained the conversation because it was of interest to him and it helped her build the relationship.

It is easiest, of course, to empathize with people who are more like us – people from a similar background, organization or culture. We click. It's therefore not surprising that connecting across government, business and society can sometimes feel like a struggle. Peter Hayes, diplomat and former Head of Public Affairs at the London Stock Exchange, has seen both sides. He comments: 'Business does not understand government's perspective and can be surprisingly naïve about government and vice versa.'

Peter's observations highlight one of the reasons why opportunities for cross-sector problem solving are limited. There is a lack of understanding on both sides and consequently a lack of trust.

We're not saying leaders shouldn't take advantage of their ability to empathize with people like themselves. But *the real value comes from understanding those who are not like us*. Understanding others with different views, from different sectors or cultures, opens up new horizons, possibilities for innovation and new opportunities.

Risk management is more robust if we learn what matters to others and bring it into decision making in business and politics. Good relationships can neutralize or diminish potential problems too. Bob Zoellick (former Head of the World Bank and US Trade Envoy) reflected that he always nurtured relations with members of congress: 'Good friends are better than troublesome enemies. You are constantly building capital for the future.'

Here's the point: it's not new but it is fundamental. Leaders who want to offer innovative, long-term and sustainable solutions in business, government and international relations must embrace a whole range of different views, ideas and contributions. We know it but we don't do it enough.

How to see and feel the others' world

Empathy is about finding echoes of another person in yourself.

(Mohsin Hamid)

Preliminary research on key stakeholders provides baseline information. However it does not tell the whole story. To fully understand someone you need to meet them, 'see the whites of their eyes', get beneath the surface and get to know the whole person, what drives them, how they like to work and which approaches they are likely to be most receptive to.

It is easier to empathize with people with whom we spend most time. Greater exposure to people provides us with more opportunities to spot patterns in what they say, tone of voice, body language and behaviour. It is estimated that we transmit 70–90 per cent of all information about ourselves through our body language. Whatever the percentage, it is a significant part of the way we communicate and reveals much about how we and others are experiencing reality.

PQ leaders are generous with their time and like getting to know people. They are curious and genuinely believe other people are as interesting, and even more interesting, than themselves. Sir Richard Branson sums it up well: 'Having a personality of caring about people is important. You can't be a good leader unless you generally like people. That is how you bring out the best in them.'

By being curious and asking lots of open questions and listening, PQ leaders gain a deeper understanding and appreciation of others – what matters to them, what they want, what their context is and what their pressures and constraints are.

Listening

We mentioned listening above. It's essential for empathy. The best leaders are great listeners. They put huge amounts of energy into being 100 per cent attentive, concentrating on reading all the verbal and non-verbal cues. They note what is said, as well as what is not said. Peter F Drucker, management consultant, educator and author, observed: 'The most important thing in communication is to hear what isn't being said.'

Hearing the unsaid requires us to listen intently for the small hesitations, the questions that go unanswered and the point that is skimmed over. Listening well involves using open questions such as 'tell me about that' and 'what else', or, just as important, it is about knowing when to be silent.

Using silence well is a skill. Handled badly it can be intimidating, as if you are waiting for a child to account for their actions. Handled well, it is generous and respectful. It offers the other person the space to reflect and speak freely, without interruption or judgement. It offers the listener greater understanding because the person will feel at ease enough to disclose more.

You can reinforce the message that you're interested and want to fully understand by techniques such as:

- summarizing what you hear;
- checking in with the other person to find out whether you've understood them correctly.

Perceptual positions

Most people are capable of sympathy and concern. If we see someone in need, we'll help them. If someone is troubled, we'll try to comfort them. Much rarer and tougher to do is empathy – the ability to feel and understand how life truly is for someone else.

Empathy requires the ability to move perceptual positions. The best leaders (and possibly, if the primate research is correct, alpha male chimps) are able to unconsciously move perceptual positions. They seem innately programmed to pick up all the subtle signals that provide insight into the world of others.

For most leaders moving perceptual positions is not innate. One of the most effective techniques for building this capability comes from neuro-linguistic programming (NLP).

Figure 6.1 explains the three NLP perceptual positions.

FIGURE 6.1 NPL perceptual positions

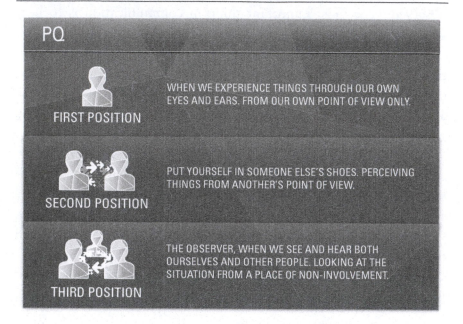

First position: this means we are in our own skin, going about our everyday business, experiencing the world first hand and responding in a way that makes sense to us. We are in the moment, fully associated with everything that is going on around us. It is how we should be most of the time.

To empathize, we need to be able to shift to *second position* and temporarily experience the world of another, so we can appreciate their reality.

There are lots of ways in which you can increase your ability to move to second position. For example, try starting with body language; as mentioned earlier around 70–90 per cent of all communication is in our body language. Here are some top tips:

Top tips

By observing closely and trying out another's body language we can access their world and with practice will get closer to understanding how they think. Try out some of these techniques:

- Try standing like the person you want to understand.

- Then walk like them and you will start to pick up clues about their energy levels, whether they are at ease or tense.

- Try out any mannerisms and notice what this tells you.

- Try imitating the way they speak, the words they use, the phrases they love, tone and vocal punctuation. What does this tell you? For instance, people who speak quickly may be enthusiastic or they may be nervous.

There are similarities between this and the approach used by method actors, who consciously move to second position so as to more fully connect with the character they are playing, as in Daniel Day Lewis's Oscar-winning portrayal of President Abraham Lincoln.

And finally there is a *third position*, when we step back and see Positions 1 and 2 from a disassociated, neutral or 'third eye' perspective. From here we can analyse what is going on for both ourselves and the other person, and then consciously think about what needs to happen to take the relationship forward.

This may require a change in our behaviour that links directly with the PQ facet 'versatility', where you need both the mental and behavioural flexibility to shift the way you work and relate. The somewhat uncomfortable truth is that sometimes, when we shift position, we realize that we are the block to progress!

Moving perceptual positions may sound complicated but with practice can become second nature. Matthew Kirk, Head of External Affairs at Vodafone, describes this ability at an organizational level as the ability to read 'the heartbeat of how accountable institutions work, the emotion of decision making'.

Do things that stakeholders value

Developing a shared relationship with key stakeholders requires you to build rapport and do things for them that they value. As one PQ leader told us, it helps if you like people and like getting alongside them. You can move from the transactional to being able to build rapport and a relationship.

Why rapport?

The purpose of building rapport is to move a relationship quickly to a position of confidence and mutual trust. We do this by:

- demonstrating empathy;
- emphasizing what we have in common; and
- doing things for the other person that they will value.

Simon Manley, British ambassador to Spain, comments that 'the best ambassadors get under the skins of the host, in a way that is different'.

Mark Sedwill, former NATO Civilian Representative in Afghanistan, said that he built credibility and acceptance with the military and NATO diplomats by sharing information, visiting each NATO force in its own area, making time to talk to the foreign media from each country, and 'showing I was there to work with them'.

Demonstrating empathy

We've discussed how to develop and use empathy earlier in this chapter. So we won't revisit it but here are a few practical tips that you may find useful – see the box opposite.

Common interests and values

Emphasizing common interests and values enables us to connect more easily with others. By highlighting shared values and interests we map out the space where we might work well together.

In a PQ context, this means connecting with other leaders and stakeholders who can help achieve a shared goal. For example, we highlighted the B Team in Chapter 4, Futurity; it is a partnership of leaders with shared values and a common aim.

When there is discord, this shared understanding of common interests helps focus effort on what everyone believes in and has to gain.

Top tips to building empathetic stakeholder relationships

1 Build rapport: Take the time to ask questions about other people and their roles, and listen with full attention. Note what matters to them and probe, go beyond the superficial conversation, dig deeper, show interest and start building connections that could be helpful. Create a climate of ease that enables you and encourages them to share and speak more openly together.

2 Keep in touch: Relationships build over time and need tending. Send occasional e-mails with articles or news that you know will be of interest. Get into the habit of arranging to meet up for a coffee or lunch when in town. Be creative; suggest activities that you can do together that you know they will enjoy.

3 Join the 10 pm list: Aim to be one of the people that this person feels they could call even out of office hours, when they have a major issue that they want to discuss and would welcome your views and support. Be there for them.

As shared interests fade, so inevitably do the partnerships that were formed around them. Finding what unites people when their interests differ is much tougher.

Value activities

What often clinches relationships is when you can do something for the other person that they value. In particular, if it helps them to achieve something that is important to them, or if it is done when they are under pressure or 'down'.

Michael Bloomberg, mayor of New York City for three consecutive terms and Bloomberg Industries billionaire, told this story to James Bennet of *The Atlantic* (2012). It illustrates the lasting impact of doing something for someone when they are 'down'.

I have always had a policy: if it's a friend and they get promotion,
I don't bother to call them; I'll see them sometime and make a joke
about it. If they get fired, I want to go out to dinner with them that
night. And I want to do it in a public place where everyone can see me.

Because I remember when I got fired from Salomon Brothers – I can tell you every single person that called me. That meant something. When I was made a partner? I have no recollection of that whatsoever.

When you help someone when there is little or nothing in it for you and everything in it for them, you build the foundations for a strong and solid relationship in almost all cases. Peter Westmacott, when British ambassador to Turkey, was door-stepped by a journalist as he came out of a hospital after visiting British casualties following a bomb attack. Asked by the reporter whether tourists should visit Turkey, he put the bombing into perspective, commenting that these incidents happened everywhere – London had 7/7 – and he would be taking his holidays in Turkey. It was just the message the Turkish authorities needed to hear at the start of the tourist season. On another occasion, he was touched to be introduced as a guest speaker 'who believes in the future of our country'. It was true, but it also meant that it was easier to deliver less welcome messages when he was instructed to do so by the British government.

When stakeholders are not under pressure but you want to build rapport by doing something they might value, you're obliged to use your empathy skills to understand what might be important to them and your creativity to think about how to do it. Here is another example from the world of diplomacy.

Example: The ambassador (II)

Here is another example from Lord Kerr's time as British Ambassador to the United States.

I actively built relationships with politicians across the United States, and consciously did not limit my network to Washington. At weekends I would visit different parts of the country.

On a Sunday, I would call on a local governor or senator. Coverage of those meetings usually led the local network news in the evening, because, of course, Sunday evening is a quiet time for political news.

The value: The TV coverage provided good publicity for the local politician that he/she valued. Lord Kerr laid the groundwork for building a longer-term relationship.

You could describe empathy as the alchemy of PQ. It's the ingredient in relationships that builds trust and shared understanding. Often those two things make the difference between success and failure.

Relates to wider society; culturally competent and respectful

Cultures are an expression of beliefs, values and deeply held assumptions that influence the way people, organizations and nations behave. PQ leaders are curious about and understand other cultures – through being well informed, travelling, job assignments, learning foreign languages and customs, and by encouraging diversity in their work places. They are fluent at the level of both organizational and international culture.

Those who are able to relate to wider society can move between different groups of people and different countries and build relationships because they are flexible enough to be able to understand how others think and feel. This is particularly important when as a leader you are in a partnership that is multi-cultural and/or brings people together from different disciplines.

PQ leaders see the opportunities that come from bringing different cultures together, to inspire new ways of thinking. They also appreciate the similarities across cultures, so easily overlooked as we tend to scan for difference.

Emphasizing shared values and the shared future vision when working with partners and stakeholders, leaders seek common ground to establish relationships and then progress to explore new and more effective ways of working together.

Culturally competent leaders understand what underpins a culture: the beliefs and values, and therefore what matters to people from that culture. They acquire this insight by studying the history of a country and its customs, by observing closely the way people relate, and for long assignments by learning the language. Speaking the language enables ease in communication, shows respect and means that these leaders are more likely to be included in the conversations at the margins of meetings and conferences (so often where relationships are built).

Thought worlds

Matthew Kirk, Head of External Affairs at Vodafone, describes people from different sectors and nations with a range of perspectives as coming from different thought worlds. Each world bumps into the others as stakeholders come in and out of contact. Each has its own set of assumptions about the other worlds.

Governments and regulatory bodies might assume the private sector is only motivated by making profit, and they do not try to understand what might incentivize business to achieve what they want.

When business people meet politicians, they tend to focus on a set of arguments around their own interests and may not always acknowledge the political or practical issues that surround it.

Matthew believes PQ leaders have the ability to build empathy across thought worlds.

PQ leaders use this insight to find new ways of working that will get them more 'in step' with the other culture. So what does this mean for leaders in international partnerships? It means that PQ leaders understand the key cultural values that underpin a culture; for example, in the East the focus is on relationships and in parts of Asia saving face, while the West is more analytical and direct.

Riding the Waves of Culture (1998), by Fons Trompenaars and Charles Hampden-Turner, provides analysis and deep insight into culture and how to think and behave in ways that respect the values of all stakeholders, and is a 'must read' for those new to international work. They conclude that the essence of cultural difference is the way people interpret the world.

Organizational culture

Just as countries have distinct cultures, so do organizations. Partnerships across organizations thrive when empathy goes beyond simply observing behaviour and making assumptions. PQ leaders dig deep and get beneath corporate behaviour to understand the corporate culture.

There is a presumption that internationalization will create or at least lead to, a common culture worldwide. The commonality would make the life of international managers much simpler. People point to McDonalds and Coca-Cola as examples of tastes, markets, and hence cultures becoming similar everywhere. There are indeed, many products and services becoming common to world markets. What is important to consider, however, is not what they are and where they are found physically, but what they mean to the people in each culture... The essence of culture is not what is visible on the surface. It is the shared ways groups of people understand and interpret the world.

(Extract from *Riding the Waves of Culture.*)

How do they do this? Many of the skills for reading organizational culture are the same as for reading national cultures: listening, observing and showing respect. Researching the history of an organization, recognizing where national and corporate culture are linked and seeing the connections between the beliefs of the founders and the current leadership provide a sense of where an organization has come from and how that affects present activity.

A quick insight into corporate culture is possible by noticing, when waiting in reception, what it looks like, how people are greeted, how they talk to each other and dress.

When you partner with other organizations, in time you can ask what matters to people in the organization, how they measure success. Find out the profile of the 'stars' in this culture and why they are important. Hear the most popular corporate stories. Ask what would you have to do here to be fired?

Demonstrating empathy at an organizational level involves behaving in a way that fits with the culture. Consider dress, protocols, how you present information, ask questions and negotiate. Attention to culture indicates respect, acknowledges difference and inevitably contributes to more successful relationships and outcomes.

PQ leaders do not judge other cultures. They are curious and enjoy learning about different ways of working, embracing diversity and flowing with it.

Culturally competent leaders are able to separate the person from the behaviour. They look beyond the expressed behaviour to what drives it, and find ways of connecting at the level of values. This keeps them positive, constructive and purposeful, rather than feeling trapped and frustrated as they respond to what may appear as blocking or antagonistic behaviour. Everyone has the potential to behave in ways that may not appear helpful to others, especially when they feel that their values and beliefs are being disregarded.

Builds shared empathy by attracting others through values, behaviours and innovation

People attract other people by expressing their values. Organizations and institutions are attractive when they behave in accordance with accepted values, and when they display creativity and innovation. Attraction, in turn, builds empathy. We know this from our personal relationships and it affects how we respond in other ways too. In this section, we'll explore what it means for business and government.

In business

Businesses are operating in a global market place. They must attract a broad range of consumers, most of whom are connected to each other through the internet and social media. If we accept that the product or service offered has value – what is it that makes one business more attractive to buy from than another?

Muhtar Kent, Chairman and CEO of The Coca-Cola Company, told us of hard evidence that consumers don't just buy what tastes good. They want, as we've highlighted in earlier chapters, to know the character of the company. In the past, marketing focused on creating consumer impressions through good adverts and good products. Now, Muhtar argues, it is about creating positive consumer expressions – so people talk positively about your business among themselves.

Muhtar Kent's views are supported by evidence in the 2013 Harris Poll, which studies the reputations of the most visible US companies. The results reflect a notable shift in the public's perception of what characterizes 'great companies'. In 2011, the public valued among other things 'trust' and 'high ethical standards'. In 2013, trust is still there but high ethical standards were replaced by 'plays a valuable social role' and 'a good feeling about the company'.

Reputation

We mentioned above the Harris Poll. Johnson and Johnson is a consistently high performer. Since 2006 it has appeared, every year in the top category of most reputable brands. Between 2006 and 2011, it was ranked first or second.

What's interesting about Johnson and Johnson is that back in 1943 they set out their values, one of which was: 'We are responsible to the communities in which we live and work, and to the world community too.' This was way before ideas like 'corporate social responsibility' and 'shared value' had been invented. We cannot say that its empathy with community and its commitment to it has determined their business success, but it is notable that the company has flourished both in terms of profit and in the way it is regarded by the public.

History tells us that some visionary and empathetic leaders pioneered PQ leadership. Those companies that have maintained the ethos, such as Johnson and Johnson in the United States or the John Lewis Partnership in the UK, continue to attract employees and customers.

In government

Democratic governments get into power by attracting votes. Political leaders understand the importance of attracting their own citizens to vote for them. However, governments also need to attract people in other countries to think well of them so as to increase their influence and boost their economies. In Chapter 2, we touched upon the concept of soft power and how governments benefit from soft power tools. We'll explore some examples here.

Culture

Culture is one of the soft power tools identified by Harvard Professor Joseph Nye. Cultural assets could be described in brief as things we like and enjoy. They include sport, food, music, film, art, literature, fashion, history, education and language. We all have our own favourites and we're drawn to countries that are recognized as world leaders in these areas, as Italy is for fashion and design.

So why does this matter? It matters economically and politically. When people are attracted to a country they visit, study, work, invest, share ideas and build partnerships. All this activity creates jobs and boosts national economies.

Time spent abroad deepens understanding of other nations' values and ways of life. It builds empathy based on experiences and memories and influences the choices and attitudes of the visitors long after they have returned home. While some visitors may later become influential politicians or business leaders in their own countries, making decisions on foreign policy or where to invest, others will be influenced in their personal choices of holidays, purchases or which foreign broadcaster to tune into. They'll also tell their children about their experiences and start to influence them too.

Brands

Guy Salter knows about luxury. He's been Managing Director of luxury brands such as Laurent Perrier champagne and Aspreys Jewellers. Guy says that luxury brands create empathy and attraction to their host countries. The luxury brand market is one of the fastest growing in Asia and other emerging markets. Figure 6.2 shows the attraction/ empathy relationship between consumers and brands and how that benefits a national economy. We've used the UK as an example but you could substitute France, Italy, the United States – in fact any country with brands that attract.

Innovation

The government of Dubai understand the power of attraction better than most. In the last 30 years, Dubai has attracted global business, international finance, tourism, top-quality sport and investment to what was once desert. In 2013, Dubai officials showed a subtle understanding of how to build empathy between two nations.

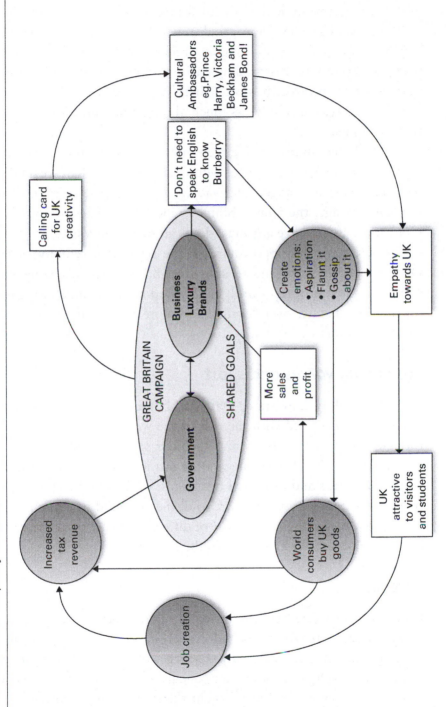

FIGURE 6.2 Empathy in action

Dubai, in a world first, became the sponsor of the Chinese national table tennis team. Table tennis is of course a huge sport in China.

It's interesting to hear how the deal was described. First by Dubai: 'We have a very strong and ongoing relationship with China. China is Dubai's second-biggest trading partner and we want to strengthen that relationship through sport.' Then by China: 'This co-operation goes beyond sport itself; it's as much about communication and cultural dialogue.'

In the United States, the big tech brands combine innovation and empowerment. Apple, Google, Microsoft, eBay, PayPal are worldwide brands that changed the way we live. And, we've all got the implicit message: the United States is the home of technology and innovation. If you have a genius idea – go to Silicon Valley.

The UK took the opportunity of the opening ceremony of the Olympics to entertain and to showcase British values, history and culture to the rest of the world. Hollywood has done much the same for the United States over decades, and more recently Bollywood has showcased India's vibrancy.

Combining values and sport

Another wealthy gulf state, Qatar, is building a shared empathy within the region and with the rest of the world through its values, foreign policy interventions and through sport. Qatar is home to the independent Al Jazeera news organization, which is valued and trusted by Arabs and respected by the rest of the world. They are to be the World Cup hosts in 2022. And, they're building a reputation as political mediators in a number of difficult international situations between East and West and within the region.

Diversity

Cultural diversity reflects the different interpretations of the world that exist between nations and cultural groups. Leaders working with international partners learn how to target their communications to fit the culture. Organizations that benefit from a more diverse workforce develop greater cultural insight through employee interactions and shared experiences.

In a global, digital media age, communications are visible to and shared across a wide community. Surprisingly often, organizational communication is targeted to the audience in the organization's host country or region. Cultural diversity helps organizations to communicate more openly and have strategies in place to differentiate communication when necessary to fit different audiences.

Inspires passion and commitment from other stakeholders to the shared project

Nothing that ever mattered was easy. Most of it is very hard. The role of the leader is to keep people focused on the shared project, especially when the project is complex and competing interests abound.

Passion

What is it that determines success or failure? Some might say vision, because it's important to see what needs to be done. Others might argue for strategy, so it gets done. Maybe, power and influence because they open doors, or trust because it binds people together.

While all of these are essential and we argue so throughout this book, what matters most is a passionate belief in achieving your goal and a strong empathy with the purpose.

Passion turns good sportsmen and women into great ones. It fuels adventurers conquering hitherto insurmountable challenges. It drives business people to create multinational empires from nothing. It sustains humanitarians working with victims of disaster and conflict. It's the invisible fuel for success.

For leaders working across agencies and with different partners to achieve their joint aims, it's harder to create this sense of commitment. What makes it difficult is that each partner brings their own identity – their own culture and values and their own way of doing things. You can overcome this when you promote and get commitment to the cause.

PQ leaders are committed to delivery and have a strong empathy with the overall mission. It drives them. And it enables them to inspire a similar empathy in others. Half-hearted partnerships cannot survive tough times. A passion for the shared endeavour is the fuel that provides drive, determination and the will to succeed.

Example: London Olympics 2012

Lord Seb Coe, who led the team organizing the London Olympics, was formerly a double gold Olympic athlete and is a passionate advocate for the Olympic Games. He was also determined that London would put on a great games that was fitting of a great city.

Organizing the Olympics in any country requires the highest PQ leadership skills. The challenges are complex and multi-dimensional and so are the stakeholders. Changes of government, changes of budget, massive infrastructure development, security, staffing, transport, with a fixed deadline and the eyes of the world on you.

The London Games faced its share of challenges, not least when the private security firm failed to deliver the trained personnel needed and the military had to step in at the last moment.

What shone through it all was the determination to make it work, to put on an event that would be worthy of its name. As one of the 70,000 volunteer games-makers said: 'Whether it was troops and police or volunteers, here were real people trying to do their bit to help.'

Lord Coe's personal commitment to the shared endeavour that had inspired the whole team was evident from his words at the closing ceremony:

> On the first day of these games I said we were determined to do it right. I said these games would see the best of us. On this last day I can conclude with these words: when our time came, Britain, we did it right.

Inspiring commitment to the shared project

Leaders create commitment in many ways but there are some common themes. They include:

- clarity about the mission;
- instilling fear; and
- good communication across projects.

Clarity of mission

Clarity of mission involves all stakeholders sharing the same understanding of the future vision and the strategy for implementing it. Many of you will know this story. But it's worth repeating as it sums up this point neatly. President John F Kennedy was visiting the NASA Space Station and he came across a cleaner and asked him what his job was. He replied 'to put a man on the moon'.

A large multinational company that aims to make profit and do it in a way that people living in local communities accept needs the same clarity of mission. Employees need to understand the what (making money) and the how (doing it with the full engagement of the community) to be able to make the right day-to-day decisions.

A local government authority tasked to work with local business to create jobs must ensure that employees understand how their specific job fits with the overall purpose. Otherwise the people may not prioritize business-friendly practices when deciding on planning applications, parking permits, waste collection etc.

In large public sector organizations, well-intentioned people can lose sight of their purpose. Bob Zoellick (former Head of the World Bank, and US Trade Envoy) comments: 'Educated people can spend hours analysing themselves and can be quite insular. You need to remind people of the mission and they need to believe in it and be focused on it.' The mission is what gets people up in the morning wanting to work and play their role. Very few people get out of bed because they are inspired to deliver shareholder return! Aligning profit and societal benefit makes a more compelling offer.

In a PQ context there is scope for ambiguity. For example, a business that balances making a profit with doing so in a way that is sustainable may face choices in the short and medium term that are difficult to resolve because in the shorter timeframe the two aims may be in conflict.

It's the leader's role to explain the purpose and the relative priorities in as many different contexts as possible and using context-specific language. Take, for example, cuts in a non-profit organization's expenditure. 'Cuts' is the language of business. The term does not land well for those with a vocation; 'treating twice as many people for the same expenditure' might.

Recognize the necessity of frequent messaging. A top political adviser once counselled: 'You must repeat your message so often that you feel if you say it one more time, you'll be physically sick, and only then may you just have said it enough.'

Fear

Fear focuses attention. Setting out the problem starkly helps people to understand the consequences of failure. We see this approach all too often with humanitarian tragedies when aid agencies are seeking funds to avert further death and disease.

Jamie Oliver is a PQ leader. He's also a highly successful chef, entrepreneur, TV presenter and author who combines his commercial business with his desire to improve people's lives. Passionate about food and people, he combines his commercial interests with his aim of making people's lives better. In the UK and the United States, he's launched campaigns to teach people how to cook, to improve school dinners and to encourage the food business to behave more responsibly. He's achieved remarkable results.

Jamie is a seasoned TV performer and a smart communicator. When he was awarded the prestigious TED prize in the United States, he took the opportunity to put his case to an invited audience of US movers and shakers. His speech was emotionally passionate, data rich and at times engagingly funny. He started by using some scary messages to grab his audience's attention. See the box opposite for an extract from the beginning of the speech to show you how it works.

Enabling good communication

In a shared power world, there are multiple stakeholders from a range of backgrounds. We heard continuously throughout our research of the failures in communication between business and government and vice versa. Neither understands the other or knows how to get the best from the other. What to ask for and what to offer. We heard the same message repeated from local businesses and government officials and from senior diplomats and CEOs of major organizations.

Jamie Oliver focuses audience attention at the TED Awards

My name is Jamie Oliver, I am 34 years old… and for the last seven years I've worked fairly tirelessly to save lives in my own way. I'm not a doctor; I'm a chef; I don't have expensive equipment or medicine. I use information and education. I profoundly believe that the power of food has a primal place in our homes, that it binds us to the best bits of life.

We have an awful reality right now.

America, you're at the top of your game. This is one of the most unhealthy countries in the world.

Can I please see a show of hands for how many of you have children in this room today? Please put your hands up. Aunties and uncles as well. Most of you. OK.

We, the adults of the last four generations, have blessed our children with the destiny of a shorter lifespan than their own parents. Your child will die 10 years younger than you because of the landscape of food that we've built around them. Two-thirds of this room, today, in America, are statistically overweight or obese.

Fact: Diet related disease is the biggest killer in the United States, right now, here today. It's a global problem (Oliver, 2010).

(The full podcast can be found on http://ented.babblebuzz.com/tag/jamie-oliver.)

A UK Regional Trade director told us that he found business people reluctant to ask politicians for what they need, especially when they are in meetings with other businesses. Although everyone has the same aim of regeneration and economic development, in the moment, confident business leaders appeared unsure how to proceed.

Former top diplomat Lord Jay says: 'It is not just a lack of trust on both sides, there is often a complete lack of understanding on both sides. There needs to be a constant relationship over time with the people who matter. Not just in a crisis, so that you get to understand each other.'

PQ leaders understand the importance of good communication with the people involved in the shared project. Creating the conditions for honest conversations between partners is essential when projects are interdependent. Without these conditions, people don't ask others for what they want or what the shared project needs.

To give you an example of the type of complexity involved, Power Africa is a series of interdependent projects working towards a future vision. Standard Chartered is financing the project to the tune of \$2bn. The US government is providing \$7m. Partners include six African governments and various US government agencies.

The project is designed to provide access to 10,000 megawatts of cleaner, more efficient electricity and give power to 20 million homes and businesses. Successful delivery of the shared project will be transformative. More than two-thirds of sub-Saharan Africa is without electricity and more than 85 per cent of those living in rural areas lack access.

During the life of the project, it's inevitable that governments will change, personnel will move on, cross-border difficulties and local community issues will emerge. Some risks will be managed by Standard Chartered working with other partners to introduce best practice for infrastructure development in Africa. But most will need to be managed by the leaders forming the partnership. How well they relate to each other and the quality of their communication will significantly contribute to the effectiveness of the projects in delivering the overall vision.

Feels an empathy with humanity and acts to make the world a better place for future generations

> We make a living by what we get and we make a life by what we give.
>
> (Winston Churchill)

Throughout history, people have worked for the good of others at all levels of society. That's not new, and it continues today in the work of many philanthropists, business people and former politicians.

PQ leaders care about the world they live in and the world they will leave behind. They feel personally responsible to work and behave in ways that will create a legacy to 'future-proof' the planet. They are clear about their role to deliver success for their organization, yet they believe it is possible to do so and make the world a better place.

Feeling responsible towards humanity is not the same as traditional corporate and social responsibility (CSR), so often an adjunct to core business. PQ leaders are zealous about improving people's lives and sustaining the planet. It's integral to their work.

Empathy and humanity

Various pieces of research have made connections between a high level of personal empathy and a desire to reach out and help people in different social groups, to resist bullying and fight inequality. A seminal study by Samuel and Pearl Oliner found that people who rescued Jews during the Holocaust had been encouraged at a young age to take the perspectives of others.

The internet, TV and travel all contribute towards presenting us with a better understanding of what is happening to people across the world. Understanding the pressures and the inequalities across our global community affects the way we all perceive the world. Whether we consider ourselves fortunate or whether we feel neglected by the world community, how we feel shapes what we do.

Knowing what is going on across the world encourages us to feel empathy with humanity and to use that empathy to inform what we do and how we do it. Mary Robinson, former UN Commissioner for Human Rights, says:

> Human dignity evokes an empathy with the other, connects us one to the other. Empathy is extraordinarily important in family, in community, in country, at so many different levels. Now, in our interconnected world, that empathy must expand to tackling the gross inequalities that raise important issues of justice (Robinson, 2013b).

Cultural historian Roman Krznaric (2012) suggests we can cultivate empathy throughout our lives – and use it as a radical force for social transformation. The challenge he identifies for social media is to move beyond passing on information (to get people out on the streets) and to forge an empathetic connection that changes behaviour.

Empathy with future generations

> Leadership is about doing what you think is right and building a constituency of support behind it. It's not doing a poll and following from the back.

Michael Bloomberg, in his fourth term as New York Mayor, made this statement and has backed it up by tackling long-term issues such as confronting the US gun lobby, limiting the sale of sugary drinks and supporting sustainable initiatives. It's always politically difficult to tackle issues that infringe on people's right to choose the way they live. Courageous leaders who have empathy with future generations see beyond the present into the future. They see what inaction now will mean for subsequent generations, and they act.

Most leaders in business and government are parents or grandparents. Society needs more of them to make the connection between what they do now and the impact on their children and their children's children.

Conclusion

The ability to understand others' perspectives and use that insight to serve a purpose is at the heart of PQ. It's not about manipulation. PQ leaders recognize that integral to their role is helping their community and society to solve their biggest challenges.

In a shared power world, building great relationships with a diverse range of stakeholders is a leader's job. The most successful businesses, nations and NGOs will attract others to support them through their values and behaviour.

Navigating around complex relationships, competing interests and a globally connected world requires leaders with a deep understanding and respect for others' positions. They tread lightly and they bring others with them.

Developing a sincere empathy for humanity now and in the future has the power to transform the way we lead.

Trust

07

> *Relationships of trust rely on our own willingness to look not only to our own interests, but also the interests of others.* **(PETER FARQUESON, CEO HABITAT FOR HUMANITY)**

What is it?

Trust is the foundation of all great relationships and the strongest determinant of their success. Trust binds relationships and enhances reputations. Behaviours that create trust include integrity, transparency, inclusivity, consistency and reliability, and concern for the best interests of others.

Ultimately all individuals and organizations are judged by their behaviour. Unlike the other PQ facets, trust is binary. People either do or do not trust you; there is no continuum for trust.

So why does trust matter in a PQ context? Leaders working in a shared power context don't have the traditional hierarchical position that gives them sole legitimacy and authority. They operate within a web of relationships, where positional power is not enough. The leaders whom others trust to serve their joint interests achieve more.

Reputation

Trust plays a significant role in reputation. How we perceive business has been a theme throughout this book. Perhaps it's not surprising that overall the tech industry enjoys the most positive reputation in the 2013 US Harris Poll. They produce the tools that enable the public to communicate with each other and access information. The poll ranks the 60 most visible companies in America, based on their reputation. Consistent top performers in the last three years were Amazon, Apple, Coca-Cola, Disney, Google, Johnson and Johnson.

We highlighted in Chapter 1 Muhtar Kent's (Chairman and CEO of The Coca-Cola Company) emphasis on the 'character of a company'. It's perhaps no coincidence then that Coca-Cola was rated the third-best company for social responsibility and fourth-best company for emotional appeal in the 2013 Harris Poll.

US Gallup polls on confidence in institutions have shown business ratings running below 20 per cent since 2006. In the UK, a Mori poll found a notable decline in the proportion of the public saying that British business behaves very or fairly ethically (58 per cent in 2011, 48 per cent in 2012). The 2013 Edelman Trust Barometer found that CEOs were globally trusted less than business by a significant margin (32 percentage points in the United States, 35 points in China and Australia and 29 points in Germany). Only 18 per cent of the general population trusted CEOs to speak the truth regardless of how complex or unpopular it may be.

John Dionisio, Chair and CEO, of AECOM, an $8bn US Fortune 500 company that has won awards for its ethical approach, comments that: 'Unfortunately it only takes one bad actor amongst the business community to taint others – especially those in the same industry as the perpetrator.' He goes on:

> As a result, besides our responsibilities to our respective stakeholders, all of us in the business community have an additional responsibility to each other in the ongoing effort to build and maintain public trust. And as we see from the Gallup polls trends, the need to go beyond the basic minimum in building trust is acute (Dionisio, 2012).

Government is trusted less than business. Government leaders are trusted much less than government according to the Edelman Barometer. In China the gap extends to 47 points, in India it is 35 points, in the United States 28 and in France 24.

NGOs enjoy high levels of trust overall. Edelman reports a notable increase in public trust in China, reflecting a wider trend across Asia. What has prompted this change? Reports say NGOs are more transparent, less critical and more collaborative with business and government, and savvier in their use of social media.

The UK Charities Commission's 2012 survey into public confidence found that overall charities enjoyed high levels of trust. But, the way in which charities use their funds is the main risk to public trust. Fifty-nine per cent of respondents said they were concerned about the proportion of funds spent on administration and salary costs. The UK Charity Commission concludes that openness and transparency and the ability to explain how expenditure and work support the cause will be essential to maintaining public confidence.

How do I do it?

The indicators of effective performance in this facet are set out below.

The indicators

✓ Consistently acts with integrity and honesty.

✓ Operates ethically, inclusively and transparently.

✓ Values and puts effort into projects and relationships that deliver long-term and societal benefits.

✓ Manages competing interests without compromising trust.

✓ Establishes a track record for consistent and reliable results.

We'll unpack these indicators in the following sections by describing the behaviours and providing examples and stories to bring them to life.

Consistently acts with integrity and honesty

The various polls and surveys on trust and confidence send a clear message to business and government leaders. Globally, trust in business is higher than trust in business leaders. Trust in government is higher than it is for government officials.

What this tells us is that there is significant business advantage or political capital to be gained by leaders who demonstrate through their behaviour that they can be trusted.

Consistency

Trusted people behave consistently. What they believe, say and do 'stacks up'. Their values and behaviours are aligned. Their beliefs run through them like lettering through a stick of rock.

This strong inner core and sense of purpose is expressed through their behaviour. They consistently model their beliefs through their behaviour at work and in their personal lives. Through their behaviour they inspire, motivate and win the support and trust of others.

Sir Kim Darroch, UK National Security Adviser, explains: 'Trust is the main building block to a successful team. The team have to trust the leader's judgement, and his honesty. And they have to believe that when he encourages them to take risks, if it goes wrong, the leader will then front up and take the blame.'

Leaders can lose sight of beliefs and values as they manage the complexity of stakeholder relationships, short-term pressures and changes in the external environment. Over time a gap may develop between their values and beliefs and what they say and do. When others notice this misalignment they start to lose confidence and trust in the leader.

How do you remain aligned? One method is to take time to reflect on your actions and decisions. Ask yourself whether they fit with your core beliefs. Is misalignment intentional? How do you feel? How is it affecting how others feel about you? For some leaders finding they are no longer aligned with the core values of their organization may prompt a move to another organization.

Honesty

PQ leaders reach out to understand the world of others by listening, observing and asking challenging questions, while indicating they are on side too. They are straight talking, use simple language and communicate clearly. They do this with ease because they are honest and not constantly covering their tracks to conceal various versions of the truth they have told over time.

Sometimes circumstances are such that it becomes tempting to offer partial information when the facts do not support a case that is important to you. Lord Kerr's (then Deputy Chairman of Shell, now Deputy Chairman of Scottish Power) advice is to resist the temptation. He says very simply: 'to build trust, you must never tell a lie. Always give the pros and the cons of every argument.'

Similar principles apply to handling mistakes. Bob Zoellick, former Head of the World Bank, recognizes that when people have worked hard and long on an important project like overcoming poverty, it's hard to admit when things go wrong. 'It's just human nature to say it could have worked, it should've worked, I really wanted it to work.' Bob used to urge his colleagues to openly acknowledge 'when it didn't work'.

Things do go wrong. Unintended consequences occur. What differentiates PQ leaders is that when they make mistakes, they do not spend their time covering things up and withholding information. They apologize quickly, and set about putting things right.

Governments often run into scandals, sometimes born of poor judgement and sometimes simply cock-ups. Jonathan Powell, former Chief of Staff to British Prime Minister Tony Blair, observes in his book *The New Machiavelli* (2011) on the lesson learned from the £1 million donation to the Labour Party by Bernie Ecclestone. The full facts will always come out in the end. 'It may seem ghastly to confess to some foolishness, and you may hope you can dribble out the details slowly, but actually doing so is counter-productive and makes you look as if you have something to hide. It is far better to opt for full transparency and get the whole story out straightaway.'

US General Colin Powell, former US Secretary of State, argues that every organization needs to be honest with itself. He tells the following story.

Story: Colin Powell

When General Powell was Secretary of State, he was responsible for submitting a report annually to Congress on trends in terrorist incidents. One year, Congressman Waxman of California accused him of cooking the books by reporting fewer terrorist incidents.

> Powell's staff defended the report – 'the traditional bureaucratic response'. But Powell instigated a review, using a military approach called 'After Action Review'. They found, as they dug deep, significant errors in the CIA categorization and counting of terrorist incidents. These errors were compounded by Powell's own staff who admitted they hadn't analysed the report adequately.
>
> Powell explains 'I called Waxman to tell him he was right and I was wrong and to assure him that my team was working hard to fix the problems and preparing an amended report. Because he trusted us he gave us the time we needed. We submitted an accurate report within a few weeks. Congressman Waxman publicly congratulated us.'
>
> (Extract from *It Worked for Me* (2012) by General Colin Powell.)

Integrity

Integrity is at the heart of trust. In this section, we'll explore integrity in different leadership contexts to see the similarities and differences between business and government.

In business

Dame Denise Holt spoke about why she felt she was appointed to be a non-executive director for HSBC Bank plc. The Chair 'knew I was happy to challenge, I am willing to speak when uneasy. Constructive challenge is helpful to a chair.'

Although the most successful leaders state that they welcome challenge, there remains lots of fear (for justifiable reasons) about being honest. The challenge therefore for leaders is be clear about the culture and climate that they want and to ensure their actions and behaviours are aligned. Jeff Bewkes showed us the boardroom table at Time Warner. It is a round table; the shape of the table is deliberate symbolism. A round table sends a powerful signal about the culture Jeff wants and the behaviour he expects.

In public policy

Democratic governments want to be re-elected, so politicians are drawn towards providing positive messages to citizens in order to win their confidence and approval. They also want to appear as if they are providing solutions to the most difficult problems facing society, and in so doing within one electoral term in office. These drivers create the conditions for short termism, superficiality and representing activity as something new when, in fact, little has changed.

It's hard to know whether the impetus for this behaviour comes from the politicians or the officials. Lord Kerr, who headed the British Foreign Office before working with Shell, believes that the current generation of UK civil servants are too inclined to allow ministers to decide without challenge. 'If ministers are wrong, officials have got to persuade them to change.'

Mathew Rycroft, COO at the British Foreign Office, reflects on the modern relationship: 'Once a relationship of trust is built with a minister, an official can then use it operationally, to advise on policy formation, to get on with implementation and to highlight risks more honestly.' Everyone agrees that it's the role of government to implement manifesto promises voted for by the electorate. This goes to the heart of the democratic system and is the foundation for trust between citizens and government.

Lord Kerr highlights the need for trust between officials and ministers. There is a tendency to want to bring good news to ministers because it's good for career progression to be well thought of by them. But just as Jeff Bewkes, CEO of Time Warner, describes lack of challenge to the boss as disastrous in a business context, Lord Kerr is clear that: 'Ministers need to know that it's straight not spinning.'

Former Head of the British Civil Service Lord O'Donnell is concerned about political short termism and the limited analysis and evaluation in the policy-making process. He wrote in the *Guardian* newspaper (2013) that: 'New ministers keen to make their mark will often rush to reverse the policies of their predecessors, or implement reforms of their own even when the evidence base is weak. This can result in a frustrating and seemingly endless state of change.' Lord O'Donnell sees academia playing a role in providing long-term evaluation that he believes will help governments tackle society's intractable problems more effectively.

Academic-led evaluation of policy will be valuable. But there is a case too for healthy relationships between politicians and officials.

Public trust in government depends on politicians and officials putting the needs of society first. Yet, the Edelman Barometer tell us that government leaders are less trusted than business leaders on their ability to solve societal issues and on their ability to make ethical and moral decisions.

The public good is served by implementing policies that effectively tackle society's most pressing problems and offer long-term benefits. Rigour and challenge from ministers and officials are essential to getting these policy projects right. Just as Jeff Bewkes, at Time Warner, creates the conditions for frank debate in a business context, so too should senior politicians and government leaders. The need for robust decision making is just as acute in government as in business.

Politically intelligent leadership is made more difficult when operating in a culture where challenge is discouraged. Perhaps one of the saddest and most tragic recent examples of this was Japan's Fukushima nuclear disaster in 2011. The investigation into the disaster concluded that the nuclear incident was 'a profoundly man-made disaster that should and could have been foreseen and prevented. The government, regulators and the Tokyo Electrical Power Co colluded and failed to provide the most basic safety requirements.' The investigators' concluded:

> What must be admitted – very painfully – is that this was a disaster made in Japan. Its fundamental causes are to be found in the ingrained conventions of Japanese culture: our reflexive obedience, our reluctance to question authority; our devotion to sticking with the programme; our groupism and insularity.
>
> (Official Report of the Fukushima Nuclear Accident Independent Commission, 2012)

On the international diplomatic stage

Trust plays an important part in international relations when negotiations are at an impasse. See the box opposite for an example.

Short termism does back-fire in international diplomacy too. Julian Braithwaite, UK Permanent Representative to the EU Political and Security Committee, describes trust as the 'holy grail'. 'EU negotiations are a repeat game. When trust is broken – when one side

---

Story: Turkey and the EU

The time was October 2005; the context was opening up accession talks between the EU and Turkey. Negotiations were taking place over the terms and conditions for accession. The UK supported Turkey's accession bid. Things were not going well.

At the end of a long day of negotiations between Turkish and EU officials in both Ankara and Brussels, the Turkish Government was poised to reject the terms that were on offer from the EU.

The UK held the rotating Presidency of the EU at the time. Sir Peter Westmacott, British ambassador to Turkey, had been closely involved throughout. Peter was summoned to the Prime Minister's office in Ankara. After a long discussion, and a final phone call from Turkish Prime Minister Erdogan to UK Prime Minister Blair, agreement was reached and negotiations could start on accession.

At a meeting a week later, the Turkish Prime Minister was asked by a visitor from London what had tipped the balance. Mr Erdogan replied 'I know Peter, and I could see from his face that he couldn't do any more for us. The phone call to Tony Blair was to ensure that the other members of my team understood that.'

Negotiations on Turkey's accession to the EU started on 1 October 2005 and are continuing at the time of this publication.

---

is seen to have reneged on a deal – reaching agreement next time is far harder.'

In Chapter 2 we highlighted the convergence towards more multilateral activity and decision making and the need for nations 'to think beyond the size of their own cabins' and prioritize the needs of society above national interest.

Martti Ahtisaari, a former President of Finland, Nobel Peace Prize Laureate and UN diplomat and mediator, is hugely experienced in international diplomacy. He feels that the emphasis has moved from the notion of rights of 'sovereignty' to 'responsibility'. He argues that: 'We have to emphasize responsibility. If we have values that we cherish, we cannot sit on the side-lines.'

Tony Blair talks about the need for statesmen rather than politicians and quotes Shimon Peres: 'A leader in office has to decide – does he want to be in the history book, or the guest book?'

Earning trust

Trust is built on honesty, integrity and reliability. People assess your trustworthiness by how you act and whether they feel you have their interests at heart.

Pierre Omidyar, philanthropist and the founder and Chairman of eBay, believes that being trustworthy and trusting others is directly correlated to business success. He believes that: 'The only thing you can do is have a certain set of values that you encourage people to adopt and the only way your customers are going to adopt those values is if they see that you're living those values as well.'

We earn the right to be considered trustworthy by our behaviour and track record. Peter Hayes, reflecting on his time as British High commissionaer to Sri Lanka, says that sometimes you have 'to show some ankle' to build trust and be seen as reliable. In other words, when we want to build trust, someone has to take the first step. This involves a willingness to both take risks and be courageous – both PQ qualities.

By making that first move we signal that we're prepared to trust, and in so doing encourage the recipient to take the next step forward in our relationship. An example of this, on a grand scale, is the Northern Ireland peace process. The road from conflict to power sharing was painfully constructed. Leaders on all sides of the political and religious divide took courageous steps forward at different points in the process to encourage and enable the other side to reciprocate.

Mark Sedwill, former NATO Civilian Representative in Afghanistan, worked alongside the US General heading NATO military forces. Reflecting on the need to build trust in key relationships in a turbulent environment, he shared his approach: 'Be very straight in private, push back respectfully. Hammer out your differences in private and be ready to compromise. Stand foursquare in public even when you don't agree. Be supportive and take the hit when things don't work out.'

Jeff Bewkes, reflecting on leadership in a shared power collaborative environment, says:

> It has to be dynamic. People come from organizational silos. You need trust. Sometimes when a leader is appointed in a new area where others know more, he or she can feel paranoid. A leader needs to have

honest conversations with people who hold different views and decide to whose judgement to trust. Who will I throw my weight behind? But the best message is: if I trust your judgment because you are the expert (and I am not), I will support you, but you are accountable. And I will learn from it.

Operates ethically, inclusively and transparently

In a shared power world, the importance of ethical behaviour and transparency increases. Leaders want to partner with people they can trust. Customers and consumers make choices based on reputation. Reputation counts in all sectors and affects how others interact with you. For example:

- In business, it determines whether consumers buy your product or use your service; whether others, including a sought-after smart innovative start-up, choose you as a partner.
- In government, it determines whether the voters will cast their ballots in your favour.
- In the non-profit sector, it determines whether donors support you.

Ethical behaviour

Most businesses understand their responsibilities to behave legally and ethically. Yet we see examples of some of the best-run businesses running into problems. Recent examples include money laundering in HSBC (Mexico) and Standard Chartered Bank (Iran). Both had come through the banking crisis with their reputations intact, only to damage them in one of their overseas operations.

Getting everyone involved to consistently apply ethical standards across a large organization is important. It's also difficult. Unethical behaviour damages reputations and destroys trust in a brand, company, cross-team collaborative project, political party or NGO.

Embedding ethical behaviour in an organization requires a leader to cover all the bases. It involves frequent communication of the organization's ethical standards and values; building ethical criteria into processes; investing in ethics training; and prizing ethical behaviour in recruitment, promotion, awards, performance management and rewards.

Even then, things can go wrong. Peter Sands, CEO of Standard Chartered Bank, reflected on this after his bank was fined by US authorities for money laundering. He said:

> We identified and introduced our values a decade ago, embedding them into our Performance Management system and rewarding people for not just what they do but how they do it. There is no single tool to reinforce culture, no magic recipe, and no organization of nearly 90,000 people can ensure that everyone does everything perfectly, all the time. But we need to keep working at reinforcing this aspect of Standard Chartered because it is one of the things that make us stand out.

Corruption

A hard challenge for businesses is when they operate in a country where bribery and corruption is widespread. While business increasingly recognizes the benefits of a 'zero tolerance' position, it is a tough choice when you operate in a market where others are prepared to use bribery and in the short term a large contract is at stake.

Mo Ibrahim, the Sudanese entrepreneur and billionaire, urges business 'to work for profit but do it with a clear social conscience and in an ethical manner'. Mo Ibrahim built his Celtel telecoms business living these values. So he knows what he's talking about.

Celtel conducted business in 14 African countries and applied ethical standards across the business. Using open and transparent procurement processes despite bribery being commonplace, Celtel's board would not approve entrance into any market unless it was clear that the licences had been obtained correctly. Many questioned whether this ethical approach was viable. Perhaps the most convincing answer is that Mr Ibrahim reportedly sold Celtel in 2005 for $3.4bn.

Jay Naidoo, a South African activist, explains why Mo Ibrahim's story is an important one for a fast-growing market (Powell, 2013):

The evidence is that Mo has become a billionaire through doing business the right way and ensuring that he never ever paid a bribe. And it sends a really good signal to anyone wanting to do business in Africa; that Africa is open for business. It's one of the fastest growing markets and we want ethical business people.

Responsible leadership

Jochen Zeitz is a smart guy. He became the youngest CEO in German history when he was appointed by PUMA at the age of 30. He turned the company from a low-priced, undesirable brand into one of the top three in the sporting goods industry. The *Financial Times* nominated him Strategist of the Year three times. Speaking on the Business Day at the UN Rio+20 conference, he observed that the private sector was often maligned for its profit motive, but in fact was the primary engine for innovation and problem solving, and he encouraged business leaders by saying: 'Our responsibility is to be accountable, ethical and responsible for our environment.'

Zeitz is not dewy eyed about business. He draws attention to companies that dump hazardous waste, use bonded labour, have negative social and environmental impacts, and have a vested interest in unsustainable development. And he warns: 'The days of companies like these are coming to an end. Transparency will become the golden rule. Business must be win–win for business and nature.'

Transparency

We'll take a moment here to reprise Jeff Bewkes of Time Warner's belief that if you have ethics, issues like transparency and rights and responsibilities fall into place. Mo Ibrahim, goes further and says: 'Lack of transparency will hurt your business.' Bono, rock star and anti-poverty activist, declared that 'transparency is the vaccine for corruption' in an interview on the influential PBS *Charlie Rose Show* (Rose, 2013).

So why does transparency matter so much? Andrew Liveris, Chair and CEO of Dow Chemicals, a $60bn US company, explains why it's important in his industry.

Building the future

> The chemical industry is still misjudged, misaligned, and misrepresented – despite the world's ballooning population and continuing globalization, both of which are making our work more exciting, more impactful, and more relevant to society than ever before.
>
> That disconnect is partially our own fault. Over the decades, the chemical industry has not done enough to operate with transparency and to lead on matters such as sustainability, spawning legacy issues that we are still resolving today.

Andrew describes the industry's evolution using what he calls 'the four Ds':

- defiance of those who called attention to problems concerning safety, pollution and sustainability;

- denial;

- debate; and now

- dialogue.

He continues:

> This experience has convinced us of the need to engage business, government, and civil society in a 'golden triangle of partnership' to set smart and effective regulations and policies. It has taught us that being a sustainable enterprise is not a digital, either/or, opt-in/opt-out exercise. It is a mandate, a key element of our license to operate.
>
> Today our industry has embraced this shift through programs like Responsible Care, a global, industry-led effort to ensure that the business of chemistry is safe, secure, and sustainable. And we are focused on innovating and commercializing products that meet humanity's needs, as well as those of our planet, enabling ample food, clean water, and smart infrastructure.

(Andrew Liveris, Extract from an article in *Chemical and Engineering News,* July 2013.)

Public policy

Bob Zoellick is a pioneer. He supports involving people in developing solutions to societal problems. See the box opposite for his example of introducing transparency into the World Bank so that data could be shared.

Opening up the World Bank

The World Bank is making openness to the public into an asset and a tool. The Bank has instituted a far reaching 'Access to Information' policy modelled on the United States and the Indian Freedom of Information Act.

All the World Bank Group's data, project information and knowledge is online – in real time and for free. The Bank has mapped all its projects so anyone with an internet connection can download the data, analyse it and come up with their own development solutions.

Bob explains: 'My aim was to "democratize development" so that a network of publics can see what the Bank is doing, add their information, and contribute to development solutions.'

Inclusivity

In a global economy with government, inter-government organizations and NGOs becoming larger and more complex in structure, organizations can appear faceless to the general public. People rarely know who works in them or appreciate the pressures they are under. This anonymity, combined with a climate of regulation, compliance and litigation, creates a rule-bound, structured environment where relationships with the public can so easily start from a position of distrust. The best organizations train customer-facing staff to balance the need for process with an inclusive approach to customers.

Politicians increasingly recognize that they should be more inclusive and transparent in the way they govern nationally and locally. Presidents and prime ministers use social media. But, more often than not, the emphasis is on broadcast rather than dialogue.

As technology develops, smart and innovative PQ leaders will create tools to develop policy in a more systematic and inclusive way with wider society. This will involve new ways of policy making. The benefits for government are more diverse thinking and more innovative solutions; and through greater inclusivity it will build understanding and trust with their priority stakeholders – voters and citizens.

Values and puts effort into projects and relationships that deliver long-term and societal benefits

This indicator of trust sits at the heart of the 'golden triangle'. It describes the behaviour of leaders who choose to put effort into projects that deliver innovative, sustainable and long-term outcomes.

Businesses that are struggling to maintain or to build public trust have a powerful incentive to partner with NGOs to deliver long-term societal benefits, as NGOs enjoy public trust. Partnering with them to deliver tangible societal benefits enhances the reputation of the business and the leader with consumers and customers.

What is encouraging is the increasing number of leaders from a variety of backgrounds who feel a responsibility to direct their skills and expertise towards delivering a better world. In this section, we share some of their stories with you.

Business

Speaking to the BBC in 2009, Mo Ibrahim provided an insight into his motivation for investing in mobile telecoms in Africa: 'The mobile industry changed Africa. We were not smart enough to foresee that. What we saw was a real need for telecommunications in Africa, and that need had not been fulfilled. For me, that was a business project, but also a political one.' Mo Ibrahim's interest in benefiting society has continued into his retirement, for example by his setting up his own foundation focused on supporting and encouraging good governance in Africa.

Bill Gates, the second-wealthiest man in the world, now devotes his time and energy to helping the neediest in society through the Bill and Melinda Gates Foundation. He explained the switch in the following terms:

I loved my work at Microsoft. It was thrilling. I devoted myself to building a company that would give us all a tool to communicate with and create in new and different ways; and that digital revolution is just beginning. Then I saw that technology does not get to those most in need and, in fact, their needs are not related to IT. They want their child to live, to have nutrition, to grow up and fulfil their potential.

International politics

A commitment to working for long-term societal benefit is alive in the world of international politics and conflict. To work on some of the ugliest, messiest and most difficult problems, Nelson Mandela set up a group called the Elders. The Elders is an independent group of global leaders who work together for human rights and peace. Although their role is that of wise counsellor rather than leader, many of their approaches mirror PQ behaviours. This is their story.

The Elders

The concept originated through a conversation between Richard Branson and the musician Peter Gabriel. The idea was simple. Many communities look to their elders to solve disputes. In an increasingly interdependent world – a global village – could a small dedicated group of individuals use their collective experience and influence to tackle some of the most pressing problems facing the world today?

They took their idea to Nelson Mandela, who agreed to support it. Mandela set about bringing the Elders together and formally launched the group in 2007. Archbishop Desmond Tutu became the first Chair.

The Elders are a group of highly experienced and influential people from across the world, with a shared commitment to peace. They work by:

- opening doors to gain access to decision makers at the highest level;

- listening to everyone, however unpalatable or unpopular, to promote dialogue;

- providing an independent voice to break taboos and highlight injustice;

- bringing people together to catalyse action and forge alliances;

- amplifying and supporting people affected by conflict or working for peace;

- creating space for campaigners and policy makers to broach difficult issues;

- connecting people with decision makers;

- highlighting neglected issues.

The Elders believe very strongly that everyone can make a difference and that everyone can achieve change in their own way.

Kofi Annan says: 'I'm often asked, what can people do to become good global citizens? I reply, that it begins in your own community.'

(Find out more at www.theelders.org.)

Manages competing interests without compromising trust and long-term benefit

In a shared power world, leaders have to find solutions that take account of competing interests. Business leaders look for ways to become more sustainable without pricing themselves out of the market. Governments face policy dilemmas between individual freedoms and protecting society. Charities balance aggressive fund-raising techniques with avoiding donor fatigue. Farmers struggle to price food competitively and maintain animal welfare standards. International organizations work with consensus and then can't act swiftly.

The leadership challenge is finding a way to meet stakeholders' short-term needs while remaining focused on delivering the long-term vision and doing it in a way that maintains the confidence and trust of society.

In business

Jochen Zeitz was challenged on sustainability by Jon Snow on UK Channel 4 TV. Jon observed (on behalf of parents of teenagers around the globe) that he could see that producing a new football strip for major football clubs every season was profitable, but asked how it was compatible with PUMA's approach to sustainability.

Zeitz acknowledged the profit point, and explained that PUMA was working on making the strips out of new degradable materials and setting up systems to enable recycling of redundant kit. PUMA's solutions were geared towards maintaining their profitable business while also protecting the planet.

When Paul Polman, CEO of Unilever, first unveiled Unilever's Sustainable Living Plan there were many who were cynical about how he could halve the carbon footprint and help the hygiene habits of a billion people while winning market share and doubling sales for a company that had long lost the habit of growing. He succeeded in pulling off the balancing act by improving performance and reducing waste. Throughout, Polman understood that without success on one side of the equation, he wouldn't have had the licence to pursue the other. Talking to the *Independent* journalist James Ashton, he said: 'If I don't have the business results, the guns will come out very quickly.'

Unilever has balanced investment in innovations like waterless shampoos and eco-friendly one-rinse fabric softeners with moving into emerging markets and selling more ice cream in hot countries! A simple addition of iron and more iodine to a Knorr stock cube balanced the business need to sell the product with providing more nutrients to help malnourished children. Polman says: 'We can solve our own issues, but at the same time we want to increasingly be using our company to be responsibly providing solutions that go a little bit broader.'

In politics

For politicians and public policy leaders, there is a balance between doing what is in the national interest and what is in the wider world interest. There is also a balance between doing what might bring short-term electoral benefit versus longer-term national interest.

One seasoned civil servant told us that what you must understand is that all politicians believe that it's in the national interest that their political party runs the country. The extension of that belief is that anything that threatens future election is not in the national interest.

So what does this mean for leaders from business, and non-profit organizations working in partnership with government? Perhaps the lessons are:

- Issues and activities will fast become liabilities if they appear to jeopardize electoral success, regardless of their intrinsic merit.

- The success of your advocacy will usually be determined by how aligned your position is with the perception of electoral success.

The following case study highlights the point. The British coalition government in 2013 was moving towards bringing in plain packaging for cigarettes. There had been consultation. The evidence was persuasive. However, the majority political party was losing support among its core voters to the more right-wing UK Independence Party (UKIP). Influential party members argued that freedom of choice trumped the health arguments and that their voters would share this view. What happened?

CASE STUDY   Plain packaging

In January 2013, the British government issued a consultation paper on moving to plain packaging for sales of cigarettes following a decision by the Australians to do so. In July 2013, they postponed the policy decision until after the next national election.
What had happened between January and July 2013?

- The politicians said 'it was an ideological issue about a free and open society' and consultation did not provide conclusive evidence that plain packaging reduced take-up – almost but not 100 per cent.

- Stripping away branding intellectual property rights could lead to compensation claims from industry.

- The ban threatens 5,500 direct jobs and 60,000 indirect jobs.

- Tobacco is a highly regulated industry but it is legal to smoke and we live in a free society.

- There is an opportunity to wait and see what happens in Australia.

- The health campaigners said: 'the decision is about politics, the profits of the tobacco industry, and less about the health of the British public' and the evidence is strong – it was set out in consultation papers and in papers from respected academics around the world. No evidence is 100 per cent.

- With every year's delay 200,000 children take up smoking and it becomes an addiction.

- Smoking kills half of all people who do it.

(Note: Policy under review again in November 2013)

What this example shows is the volatility of politics when competing interests are at play. Initially the tobacco companies had lost the argument. But when the politics changed because of the local election defeats, politics trumped public health concerns. There is a contrast here with the example of empathy with future generations shown by Michael Bloomberg in Chapter 6, page 119. In this instance the politicians prioritized those voters who don't like government interference in their lives.

Ugly choices

Tony Blair suggests leadership in 2013 was especially tough because of what he calls low predictability and a context where all the choices are ugly. He cited the debate raging between those advocating austerity and those promoting growth. No one truly knows which is right. There are strongly opposing views on whether to intervene in Syria or not. The best short-term politics will often pull in the opposite direction from the best long-term policy. Blair offers this advice (with he says the humility born of experience): 'In unpredictable times, calculation of risk and interest is hard; so, as a leader, do what you believe to be right, even if unpopular. Lead from a point of principle. Because the conventional wisdom of today may be the disposable folly of tomorrow' (Blair, 2013).

Perhaps the mark of the best leaders is that they manage competing interests because they are guided by the interests of their people.

Harvard Professor Joseph Nye, in an interview with *Der Spiegel* in 2009 (Steingart and Schmitz, 2009), offers two examples:

> Important political leaders never just followed their own interests, they were most concerned by the interests of their people. Take Nelson Mandela: he decided that reconciliation would be more important for South Africa than revenge. Or, Helmut Kohl [former German Chancellor]: he put the goal of German reunification at the top of the political agenda and was less concerned about the effects on the West German economy at that time.

International diplomacy

We live in an integrated and mutually dependent world, and this creates opportunities for partnership as countries manage their national interest and also seek to co-operate with allies. But inevitably any grouping of nations will be juggling national interest with the needs of the whole group.

In the following story of international partnerships Julian Braithwaite, explains how nations need trust for effective political relations.

CASE STUDY The Entente Cordiale

The foreign policy and defence relationship between the UK and France – at its core, the relationship between several dozen people in Paris and London – highlights the importance of trust for effective political and state relations.

Of all the countries in Europe, France and Britain are most alike when it comes to international affairs. They are the only two military powers in Europe willing and able to use force abroad, both are members of the UN Security Council, both nuclear powers, both seeking to retain a global role as the demographic and economic tide moves relentlessly against them.

With so much in common, the two countries should be natural allies in forging the future of Europe's security and its place in the world.

At a tactical level, that is often the case. From the use of force to protect civilians in Libya to supporting the opposition in Syria, Paris and London often work in concert to convince less forward-leaning EU partners of the need for action.

But strategically the promise of an Anglo-French vision for Europe's role in the world – of the scale and ambition of the historic Franco-German vision for Europe's internal affairs – has never been realized. The comparison is illuminating. The French and German elites decided after the Second World War that peace in Europe could only be secured through a decisive break with the past. In place of competition, they would collaborate, not only working together where they agreed but also supporting each other's interests even when they diverged. In short, they decided to put the much larger long-term benefits of collaboration ahead of the periodic short-term disadvantages. This required an extraordinary act of will to begin with. But it is now founded on the trust that comes from 60 years of partnership, although the euro crisis is shaking that foundation.

France and Britain, who had been allies during the two World Wars, never had the same existential reason to put aside tactical advantage for strategic gain. The UK has also had to balance its equities in the relationship that in the 20th century truly was existential: the transatlantic security relationship that secured peace and democracy in Europe in the Second World War and over the much longer struggle of the Cold War.

In the case of the relationship between France and Britain, there was not the same willingness to take risks to create mutual trust. Those who advocated doing so were more likely to be seen as outriders, misjudging their countries' true interests, rather than courageous exponents of the right course of action. Attempts to build such a true partnership often ended in disappointment, even to the present day.

The net result has often been a perception over the years – in both capitals – that the relationship lacked the integrity and reliability necessary to safeguard the two countries' most vital interests, unlike say the respective relationships with the United States and Germany.

That may be changing as the United States' attention shifts to the emerging challenges and opportunities elsewhere in the world, particularly Asia, and the balance of interests for both countries changes. The Lancaster House Treaty signed by Paris and London in 2010 is an indication of that. But even as the logic of partnership intensifies, it must be matched by an equal intensification of the trust between the relatively small groups of individuals in both capitals who manage the relationship, if it is ever to be fully realized.

(Julian Braithwaite, UK Permanent Representative to the EU Committee for Security and Peace.)

Competition or collaboration

In the non-profit world of charities, academia, public health and science, one might expect high levels of collaboration within the sector to increase the likelihood of delivering a better outcome for society. Perhaps surprisingly, that is often not the case.

Many organizations and institutions within each sector guard their own turf. Governments encourage collaboration but find that academics would rather compete. Charities working in a similar field could work together to provide better levels of service, more impactful research, specialization and centres of excellence. But many prefer to operate independently.

Today, the complexity and interconnectedness of social problems demands a shared power response in these areas as well as from government and business. While there are good examples of co-operation across different non-profit groups, for example on the UK's overarching Disaster Emergency Committee, there is scope to do much more.

What could turn competition into collaboration? First, leaders with a strong sense of mission and a passion to deliver the best outcomes for society. Second, investment in building trusting relationships between leaders and staff in organizations that currently compete and should collaborate. More than organizational design, governance and accountability arrangements, it is terms and conditions, trust and a sense of shared mission that are the two most influential factors that cut through disagreements and low-level conflicts of interest.

Establishes a track record for delivering consistent and reliable results

Reliability and consistency are as important to building trust as integrity, transparency and ethics. In a shared power world, people are mutually dependent. They rely on others to deliver what they promise.

Reliability depends on capability as well as values. Making sure that you have the necessary competences, skills and resources to deliver what you promised, at the agreed level of quality, is part of the trust equation. Evidence in recent surveys suggest that people expect competence and are rating companies as more trustworthy when they engage well with consumers or do things for societal benefit.

Competitive edge

In times of change and uncertainty, leaders who are trusted to behave reliably and consistently have an edge. People have confidence in them and are more willing to accept their direction. Time spent on persuasion and getting consensus is reduced. As you can imagine, this makes a difference, especially in crises.

Organizations and project teams that have built trust through consistency and delivery attract others to work with them. People want to be part of something that is successful and is held in high esteem by others. They know the culture will facilitate knowledge sharing, co-operation, creativity and empowerment because the focus is on delivering a good outcome rather than on internal politics or exploitation of the vulnerable.

How trust affects outcomes

The need to track and measure progress and delivery is a theme that runs through PQ leadership capability. Stephen MR Covey suggests that trust is measurable. In his book *The Speed of Trust* (2006), Covey presents a simple formula to prove his case and to shift the perception of trust as an intangible and unquantifiable variable to an indispensable factor that is both tangible and quantifiable.

Covey's conclusion is that trust always affects two outcomes – speed and cost. When trust goes down, speed will also go down and costs will go up.

$\downarrow$ Trust = $\downarrow$ Speed $\uparrow$ Cost

When trust goes up, speed will also go up and costs will go down.

$\uparrow$ Trust = $\uparrow$ Speed $\downarrow$ Cost

NGOs

Most NGOs rely on fund raising. Their reputation for reliable delivery is paramount. Donors want to know that their money will go to the cause and that it will make a difference. The general public are priority stakeholders because they support aid agencies through individual donations and as tax payers funding government donations.

In this context, NGOs must be reliable and accountable for delivering results. One of the criticisms of overseas aid is that money is used to alleviate the short-term need and in the long term nothing changes. Aid agencies justifiably would dispute this. But it is noticeable that the Gates Foundation has won the confidence of philanthropists because of its emphasis on clear targets and measurable delivery.

NGOs work with multiple accountabilities. They must satisfy donors, users of their services and regulators. Each stakeholder group has different perspectives on what reliable delivery of results means.

Demonstrating reliability and capacity to deliver is central to effectiveness. Leaders must set standards that allow transparent measurement of effectiveness and financial integrity.

Donors want to know that their money is spent reliably and not going into the back pocket of a government official or corrupt policeman. But NGO staff work at the sharp end. What do you do when you are delivering food and you can't get past a roadblock to feed hungry people without paying a bribe?

NGOs comply with the law and have ethical standards and policies in place. They partner with local agencies, and working collaboratively they can put pressure on governments and others to deliver aid effectively. But that is not easy when coping with poor infrastructure and trying to help people in remote places. News reports on delivery of aid to victims of the Pakistan earthquake living in remote parts of the country illustrated the practical challenges.

So how do NGO leaders manage public expectations and maintain/enhance their reputations for reliability when their work is generally conducted in challenging contexts? Social media and communications offer the tools. Rather than simply presenting a two-dimensional picture of making a donation and transforming a life, more forward-thinking NGOs are using digital media to show supporters and the wider public a fuller picture. Involving external stakeholders in decision making, compliance issues, evaluation and measuring impact helps understanding and reduces reputational risks in the 'court of public opinion'.

Trust and international negotiations

Sir Kim Darroch, UK National Security Adviser who is a veteran of international negotiation, emphasizes that:

> Trust is a pre-requisite for successful negotiating. The other side have to believe you when you tell them that something is completely unacceptable to your government. If they go and check behind your back and discover this was a bluff, they will never again believe anything you say. Similarly, if you say to them, 'Move this extra yard, and I'm confident that I can sell the deal in my capital', you had better deliver. If you don't, you'll never again get that extra move that brings the deal home. They have to believe that you will be as persuasive and as trusted with your own side as you have been with them.

CASE STUDY   The Lisbon Treaty negotiation

In essence, the proposed EU Constitutional Treaty had been rejected by French and Dutch voters in referenda. After a pause, the EU decided to produce a shorter, simpler, more modest set of reforms – a text that became the Lisbon Treaty.

   The British government of the day (PM Tony Blair) decided not to hold a referendum on this proposed new treaty, but to take it through parliament. But even that was going to be hugely contentious. There was a big public debate going on, so it was clear to all our EU partners that we would have a real challenge in getting it ratified and through parliament.

   As EU Adviser to the Prime Minister, I was lead negotiator on the new treaty. Basically the task was to persuade our EU partners that we could only get the new treaty through if we obtained some significant concessions, exceptions and British opt-outs; but also that, if they gave us what we needed, we were confident we could deliver British ratification.

Trust played a central role in two aspects of this. First, I had to advise the then Prime Minister on what he could ask for that was actually negotiable – so he had to trust my judgement on things we could get. Second, our EU partners had to be persuaded that if they made these concessions to us, we could deliver ratification. Some of the changes we wanted were difficult for our partners and caused political problems for them, so they had to take something of a hit for us.

In the end, they gave us what we needed, and we managed to get parliamentary ratification. It felt at the time like a huge gamble, and I can remember lying awake at night thinking of the consequences should it go wrong. It felt like walking a tightrope. And of course, *it could never have worked unless our EU partners had believed – trusted – that if they made the concessions we wanted, we would deliver.*

(Sir Kim Darroch, The UK National Security Adviser.)

Conclusion

Reputations are built on trust. Leaders build trust through behaviour. Consistently acting with integrity, being open and transparent about their actions and how they do things, they create the conditions for delivering successful outcomes.

PQ leaders across all sectors prioritize society. They create opportunities to do things that offer long-term societal benefits, and in so doing they burnish their own reputations by showing they care about others.

Welcoming openness, challenge, inclusivity and diversity, they want the broadest possible input to their projects and decisions. Championing ethical standards, they embed them in culture and behaviour.

Working in a mutually dependent context, they don't over-promise. Rather, they value their reputation for reliability and make sure that they deliver for themselves and for others.

We end this chapter with a case study from Andrew Dunnett, Group Director of Sustainability and Vodafone Foundation. Andrew joined Vodafone in 2007 and has always believed that the core business and the values of the organization are aligned. In the following case study Andrew describes how Vodafone achieved it.

CASE STUDY   Vodafone – Aligning core business and values

Companies often want their community/sustainability programmes to show and communicate something of the values of a company, and of course the local routes and commitments. This is no easy task. Whatever the sector, industry or business, communicating values in a communications age is surprisingly difficult with the multiplicity of channels and messages. People – and there are likely to be three audiences for this agenda: colleagues, customers and commentators – have trouble processing the stuff/information that companies play at them all the time. To help with that when it comes to communicating something of the deeper values through activity such as community investment/sustainability, I have found there to be three key things to bear in mind.

Firstly, companies need to link their work in this space to their core business; unless they do they have to move people from a mental deficit of 'Why are we doing this stuff?' and 'What's it got to do with our business?' Five years ago at Vodafone, virtually none of our charitable programmes were linked to our technology; now over 72 per cent have a direct link, a programme which we call Mobile for Good, and within the next year its likely to be 100 per cent. Chequebook charity is definitely a thing of the past in our company.

Secondly, you have got to do less better in this space. When it comes to the values piece the biggest danger is you just keep adding stuff; often it's all great, very well intentioned and difficult to refuse. But the more you do, the less chance you have of doing something truly transformational. Innovation is great of course, but transformation at scale is genius and that takes patient capital. At Vodafone we were moving towards 1,000 charitable partnerships across 27 countries. All good of themselves, but not really the platform for delivering something transformational at scale. Now we have max of 10 projects per market and that is still in my mind too much.

Thirdly, really asking the question 'what will we be famous for?' is a great filter. It's not why a company does this stuff. In an age of impression marketing, companies want the impressions to last; and really challenging oneself as to whether the impressions will last is another great filter for supporting and driving the right programmes.

Two leaders in Vodafone who have driven this agenda forward and inspired me in the work I do are Guy Laurence and Kyle Whitehill.

Guy Laurence CEO Vodafone UK asked his team why only Comic Relief, UNICEF and the largest charities were using text-based donations to raise millions for charity. Cost and complexity appeared to be the main barriers, so

Guy challenged them to come up with a text-based giving platform that could be used by any UK charity and fundraisers so that everyone in the UK could have their own short code for using their handset to raise money. Rather than building a platform from scratch, Vodafone UK and the Vodafone Foundation entered into a commitment with Just Giving to front-end their online portal with a text giving system. Two years on 18,000 charities and over 80,000 fundraisers have used the platform and £10 million has been raised for charity. It's totally free to use and anyone on any network can give. This award-winning programme is built on Guy's passionate belief that the next generation will give to charity via their handsets.

When Kyle Whitehill was appointed CEO of Vodafone Ghana, he asked the marketing team to put on one wall all the current above-the-line marketing activity. Then he asked them to put on the other wall all the hassles, worries and problems that Vodafone customers have to put up with every day of their lives. Access to healthcare is a huge problem, with one doctor per 80,000 people in the country. Kyle asked the simple question: If they can't see a doctor, why can't we put them on television and sponsor a programme to provide some of the health messaging that is so desperately needed? Despite initial scepticism from the team, Kyle challenged them to develop the idea and now three series of the programme have been aired and Ghana Healthline has become one of the top three TV programmes in Ghana, been a critical element of the Vodafone brand refresh in country and the local team are building the equivalent of an NHS Direct to answer the huge demand and interest that the programme has prompted.

(Andrew Dunnett, Group Director Sustainability and Vodafone Foundation.)

Versatility

08

"Coming together is the beginning, keeping together is progress. Working together is success. (HENRY FORD)

What is it?

Versatility is about having a broad range of thought and behaviour and the self-command to use it intentionally. It's responding swiftly and fully to demanding situations, knowing when to be flexible and subtle, and when to be strong and focused. PQ leaders project confidence and ease. It appears effortless but, like most things that look easy, it's challenging to master.

To explain the essence of versatility it may help to use a metaphor. Visualize a gymnast performing on parallel bars. What do you see? Flexibility, controlled movement and effortless flow, grace and ease? Now imagine what underpins this: strength, focus, discipline and preparation.

So what are leaders doing in a PQ context?

First, they're working on complex multi-dimensional problems, in a partnership and with a range of stakeholders.

Second, they're versatile: whether dealing with crises or anticipating the future; behaviourally moving up and down the scales – between firm and flexible, analytic and empathetic, vision and rigorous implementation.

Third, they understand the importance of image, symbolism and behaviour; and they make choices based on these criteria.

Fourth, and this is an overarching point, they must be masters in PQ, able to use all five facets in harmony. It's a demanding framework, requiring discipline and versatility to match behaviour and processes to the demands of the situation.

How do I do it?

The indicators

✓ Changes tack to meet new demands ranging from crisis to evolution.

✓ Exercises self-command to calibrate responses and pace change to fit the circumstances.

✓ Maintains focus and a disciplined approach, rigorous and well prepared.

✓ Exudes confidence, at ease and in touch with others' needs.

✓ Recognizes political reality, knows when to push and when to concede, and works with the politics to achieve objectives.

The following sections explore each indicator of capability in depth.

Changes tack to fit new demands ranging from crisis to evolution

New demands

Leaders who are future-focused understand that the environment is continually changing and are ready to move with it. Changes are often gradual and subtle, and frequently invisible to those involved.

Monitoring tools should be in use to spot patterns and trends indicating change early enough to allow timely evaluation and action. Change that remains undetected has the potential to derail any project, even more so when you are working within a complex landscape with multiple stakeholders on a joint endeavour.

Punctuating these evolutionary changes in the landscape are spikes of crisis that burst on to the scene and demand immediate attention. If mishandled, they too have the potential to derail any project.

Crisis

The one predictable thing about crisis is that it will happen. What's tricky is that despite leaders' best efforts to anticipate it, they don't always see when or where it will happen.

Typical examples from business are faulty or dangerous goods that are sold to consumers. In Chapter 2, we offered the Yum Inc example, illustrating how social media increases the speed of damage.

Crises blow up for governments all too frequently and the challenges are often immense. Easily recognizable examples include:

- natural disasters (tsunamis, hurricanes and earthquakes);
- aggressive actions by another state leading to conflict or an inflow of refugees;
- terrorist attacks;
- mass protests.

Evolutionary change

Evolutionary change is potentially more dangerous than crisis because, like an iceberg beneath the water, the danger isn't apparent until it's too late. The most frequent characteristics are:

- *Inherent risks* in the system that are neither addressed nor managed adequately. The risks are known, but not acted upon because there is no immediate problem and taking action is costly either financially or reputationally. Warnings are dismissed because they raise difficult decisions. Those most closely associated with the system find it hardest to see the faults.

- *The external environment* is changing. The changes could be political (eg imposition of a new tax or regulation), economic (exchange rate increases), technological (new technology renders your product obsolete, or your service can be obtained more easily online), social (changing attitudes), environmental (your product is too energy hungry). The common denominator is that if you do not adapt fast to the changing circumstances you will become increasingly irrelevant and probably face crisis. Perhaps not today, but tomorrow.

The Gulf of Mexico oil spill encapsulates both emerging risk and the white heat of crisis. In this case, both industry and government should have acted earlier. The risks associated with deepwater drilling were known, but neither BP nor the US regulatory authorities gripped them. When the rig blew, both the company and the government were engulfed by crisis. As indeed were many small businesses in the area.

Gulf of Mexico oil spill

In April 2010, the Macondo well exploded, costing the lives of 11 men, sinking the Deepwater Horizon drilling rig and spilling 4 million barrels of crude oil into the Gulf of Mexico. The investigative report into the disaster said:

> The explosive loss of the Macondo well could have been prevented. The immediate causes of the Macondo well blowout can be traced to a series of identifiable mistakes made by BP, Halliburton, and Transocean that reveal such systematic failures in risk management that they place in doubt the safety culture of the entire industry.

> The oil and gas industry, long lured by Gulf reserves and public incentives, progressively developed and deployed new technologies, at ever larger scale, in pursuit of valuable energy supplies in increasingly deeper waters, farther from the coastline.

> *Regulators, however, failed to keep pace with the industrial expansion and new technology – often because of industry's resistance to more effective oversight.* The result was a serious and ultimately inexcusable shortfall in supervision of offshore drilling that played out in the Macondo well blowout and the catastrophic oil spill that followed.

Changing tack in a crisis

Let's start by exploring how leaders respond to crisis. One of the deciding factors in how well a crisis is managed is how quickly you recognize the crisis for what it is and take action. That seems obvious in the cold light of day. But, in crisis, leaders are often paralysed by disbelief and a very human reluctance to accept that something seriously bad is happening. Inevitably this leads to delay in taking timely action.

Jonathan Powell, Chief of Staff to British Prime Minister Tony Blair during 10 years of government, reflected:

> There seems to be a pattern to crisis management. First is the failure to realize how serious the crisis is. Then comes the panic. There is also a grim pattern to the statistics, brought home to me by the Tsunami in 2004. Initial reports indicate relatively small numbers of deaths, but the numbers start increasing dramatically after a few hours and then continue growing in the days following. In the end, you usually end up with a number that is a bit higher than the initial estimate but much lower than the enormously inflated figure on offer a few days after it took place. The same pattern held true for 7/7.
>
> (Powell (2011) *The New Machiavelli*)

Working with partners and stakeholders necessitates clear communications, initiating joint work fast to establish the extent of the impact and start finding solutions. Your ability to move quickly and effectively to joint problem solving is determined by the quality of your relationships and the level of trust between you.

Top tip

When facing a potential crisis, Jonathan Powell's advice is that 'it is better to err on the side of over-reaction than under-preparation'.

Changing tack: evolutionary change

It's almost counter-intuitive to think about threats and risks when things are going well. *Internally*, leaders collect robust operational data so they can see the early signs of changes in growth and activities, reflect with partners on what that means for delivering the overall vision, and manage resulting changes in strategy, resource allocation and impacts on staff and stakeholders.

Externally, leaders avoid blind spots by staying well informed through their networks, scanning the horizon for changes in the environment, monitoring social media and encouraging and fostering innovation.

The key PQ differentiator is to use the detail of today and work out what it means in the future landscape. Ask the following questions:

- What does the future want and need from our organization/ partnership?

- Who are the best people to deliver it?

- Can we do it?

- What are the risks to existing ventures that are hovering on the horizon?

- How might these be managed?

By asking these questions when performance is strong, we initiate new thinking and innovation at the high point of the performance curve, allowing time to prepare contingency plans or new ventures ahead of requirement.

Clayton M Christensen, the thought leader on disruptive technology and author of *The Innovator's Dilemma*, notes examples of products that have been overtaken by innovation (personal computers replacing mainframes, smartphones replacing personal computers, online trading taking business from department stores). He predicts more radical change, possibly in areas where there is reliance on advertising revenue or where there are free or cheap, good-quality online resources becoming available that might replace existing products or services.

Underpinning the importance of PQ, his latest thinking on innovation (*New York Times* article, 3 November 2012) is linked to empowerment and delivering societal benefits. He suggests:

- *Business leaders* should think about transforming complicated and costly products for the benefit of the few into cheaper, simpler products for the benefit of the many, and in so doing also create more jobs.

- *Public policy leaders* should think about restructuring taxation to reward those that innovate in a way that empowers others rather than sitting on capital.

Range

What we're learning here is that a leader who works with multiple stakeholders needs more than the usual range of behavioural flexibility. Operating in a context of shared power and complex relationships generates new situations and different challenges to running your own operation.

TABLE 8.1 Core skills for crisis and evolution

Core skills: Crisis	Core skills: Evolutionary change
• Act quickly.	• Imagining the future.
• Set priorities.	• Observant. Noting the most subtle of changes in context and the behaviour of others.
• Engage with the full range of stakeholders. Visit scenes of crises.	• Networking.
• Keep the media onside by meeting their needs.	• Gathering information – questioning and listening.
• Problem solving.	• Assessment and evaluation.
• Focus on the facts.	• Encouraging challenge and innovation.
• Decisiveness.	• Investing in research and planning so as to prepare for different eventualities.
• Openness and inclusivity – never covering up, even when this provokes criticism by alerting other stakeholders to your own failings.	• Explaining future context.
• Encouraging others to find solutions – using all the talents available.	• Winning support from stakeholders.

While some problems will arise within your own area of activity, they may also surface in partners' activities. Dealing with problems on home territory feels more comfortable because the lines of authority are known and understood. Working to resolve issues working with and through partners requires different skills. See Table 8.1 on page 173 for some ideas on the core skills grouped by crisis and evolutionary change.

When leaders work with and through others to make complex decisions, their role is threefold:

- explain the context;
- develop the vision; and
- get the support of other stakeholders, most of whom have their own set of constraints to manage.

This is when the PQ capability framework harmonizes all five facets. You bring into play:

- *futurity* to re-set strategy, manage the risks and maximize the opportunities;
- draw on *empathy* with purpose to explore and understand others' positions and maintain commitment to the joint endeavour;
- use the *trust* and credibility you have built to maintain support in difficult times and get others to work with you;
- utilize your *power* with essential stakeholders to make something happen that helps you make the necessary changes;
- focus on the *future vision* while being versatile enough to respond tactically to the needs of others without putting at risk long-term goals.

When Virgin Rail lost the UK West Coast franchise, Sir Richard Branson employed a range of PQ skills to turn the threat to the survival of his company into an opportunity for further growth.

CASE STUDY   Sir Richard Branson challenges the UK government

In August 2012, Virgin Rail (a partnership between Virgin and Stagecoach) lost the UK West Coast Rail franchise that it had operated since 1997. The company faced extinction.

Focus

Sir Richard Branson stepped up to the challenge. A charismatic character with a big story, he quickly got mass media coverage and used media appearances to ask the Prime Minister to intervene. He described the bidding process as insane and drew historical parallels, making the link between the West Coast train line franchise decision and the disastrous East Coast franchise, which led to two successive franchisees handing back the keys after making overly optimistic bids.

Character of the company

Over 140,000 people signed an e-petition asking the government to reconsider its decision. The petition was started by a rail passenger who was independent of the company. He said: 'I can't think of a time when so many people have rallied around a private company. The impression I've always had is that they're good people to deal with and that means something to customers, even if it doesn't mean anything to the Department for Transport.'

Calibration

Branson was flexible, offering to help the government manage the process by running the franchise on a non-profit basis to allow time for review. But when the UK Minister for Transport supported his officials and the franchise decision, Branson recalibrated and launched legal action, taking the Government's decision to judicial review at the High Court.

The Government response was initially to defend the action. But three months later its case collapsed when significant flaws in the procurement process were admitted. Branson and Virgin Rail were vindicated. Virgin later had its West Coast contract extended to April 2017. It also confirmed its intention to bid for the next East Coast train franchise. Quite a turnaround for a company facing extinction nine months earlier.

Persistence

After the extension, Branson wrote in his blog: 'Our lawyers said we had less than a 10 per cent chance of winning after the Government originally awarded the franchise to First-Group. One of the key things we have learned is never to give up, if you think that right is on your side.'

Exercises self-command to calibrate responses and pace change to fit the circumstances

Calibration

PQ leaders are operating in complex environments. Self-command is necessary in order to calibrate responses to get the pitch right and move at a speed that brings others with you.

When crises happen, irrespective of the size of your operation, pressure mounts from a number of sources: for example, intense media interest, special interest and lobby groups spotting an opportunity to further their cause, and local or national politicians making political capital. Partners and powerful stakeholders with influence that dictates the success or failure of a joint project need reassurance.

It's often at these moments, when the stakes are high because of the scale of investment or because political reputations are at risk, that people overreact and start looking for someone to blame. Resisting the desire to criticize or undermine others is essential because any hint of division among stakeholders will be seized upon by other parties such as shareholders or the media. Situations easily spiral out of control, causing damage to individuals, organizations and institutions.

Knowing that, in tense situations, every word, gesture and facial expression is analysed by others, leaders aim to calibrate their responses to produce the best possible outcome.

Some do it by withholding all emotion. You'll see them on the media appearing very stiff and analytical. You'll have noticed that it doesn't work because we all, whether stakeholders, staff or customers, want to see empathy and sensitivity to the human aspects of the crisis.

Other leaders succumb to the magnitude of their own feelings and say or do something unwise that haunts them.

Example: Tony Hayward and the Gulf of Mexico

Tony Hayward, then CEO at BP, during the Gulf of Mexico oil-spill crisis miscalibrated and shared how he was feeling after weeks working under pressure. He commented in an interview that he would 'like his life back'. People living along the coast who had lost their livelihoods as a direct result of the oil spill, environmentalists heartbroken by the damage to marine life, and many politicians reacting to voters' concerns were incensed by this statement.

On one level, Tony Hayward was simply saying how he felt, but on another he was failing to show that he understood the damage that had been inflicted on others who unlike him had no opportunity to take action to prevent or mitigate the risk of an oil spill.

Tony Hayward then took a couple of days out to see his son for six hours. He miscalibrated again and, instead of seeing him in the privacy of his home, he went to see him at the annual yachting regatta in Cowes, Isle of Wight, a major high-society and celebrity event. The media found out and he was portrayed as taking time out to hang out with the rich and famous instead of sorting out the crisis.

In fact, Tony Hayward was working round the clock to find a solution to the oil spilling into the ocean. Taking a short break with his family would, in all likelihood, have helped him gain perspective and bring a fresher sharper mind back to the problems. But that wasn't how it appeared.

The price of the two miscalibrations was that Tony Hayward came under more pressure. He and BP suffered further reputational damage over and above that already caused by the oil spill. Not long after he was replaced as CEO.

Self-command

Having the self-command to calibrate our responses appropriately is driven by three things:

- in part, our own personality and how well we deal with pressure;

- the quality of our relationships with key stakeholders, which will determine the level of support we get; and

- our ability to read the mood of different stakeholders and say what is needed.

Self-command is essential to choosing the right response to a situation. Daniel Goleman (the recognized thought leader on Emotional Intelligence, EQ) talks about 'self-regulation'. He includes it as one of the EQ competencies and describes it as 'the ability to control or redirect disruptive impulses and moods' and 'the propensity to suspend judgement, to think before acting'.

Goleman argues that the hallmarks of self-regulation are trustworthiness and integrity, openness to change and comfort with ambiguity. The first three fit with our findings. Comfort with ambiguity in a PQ context is reframed as comfort with complexity and shared power relationships. We would add a link to being courageous – doing what is necessary and right for the present and critically for the future.

Having the self-command and coolness to wait when others are pressing for action, or to act when others are dithering, requires courage and integrity (Goleman, 1998).

Association and disassociation

PQ leaders have the capacity to associate and disassociate from feelings. To clarify what this means, it's worth taking a moment to define what we mean by association and disassociation. Association is when we are really into something, connected with it and feeling it. Disassociation is when we are detached from something, able to stand back and be objective.

So to use some familiar expressions, a 'hot headed' person is in an associated state, feeling strong emotion; a 'cool head' is disassociated and able to be dispassionate. PQ leaders normally have enough self-command to choose their state to fit the needs of the situation.

Remember the Bill Gates example in Chapter 4: passionate about the cause but dispassionate about the data.

Disassociation

We saw in the Tony Hayward example the risks of being disassociated from the emotional impact of a situation – appearing self-oriented and not empathizing with others. However, at other times it is necessary to stand back and get perspective, assess the situation, identify priorities, risks and opportunities, and put a plan into action.

Disassociation brings benefits such as helping manage well-being in times of crisis by carving out time to eat and sleep so as to maintain energy and judgement. It's important in periods of continuous stress to allow the mind space to get a mental break from pressure through meditation, yoga, running or whatever activity fits the situation and works for you. The objective is to create space for the mind to refocus.

Mark Sedwill, former NATO Civilian Representative in Afghanistan – which is the equivalent civilian rank to the four-star general running military operations – noted how easily he could have worked 24/7 because of the pressure of work and being away from family. So he made it a rule to take Friday morning and two evenings a week off.

Association

Being in an associated state is important when visiting scenes of crisis, and for communicating with stakeholders as you seek to understand how they are feeling and walk in their shoes. Sometimes really understanding how others are feeling or suffering can be deeply emotional. And even the most skilled leaders find their emotions rise to the surface.

Mary Robinson, former President of Ireland and ex-UN Commissioner for Human Rights, is someone who values her self-command. She tells this story about how she lost her composure and was more compelling as a result.

Story: Mary Robinson in Somalia

Mary Robinson visited war-torn Somalia during her term in office as President of Ireland. After the visit she gave a press conference in Nairobi.

I was very much under control during a harrowing visit, even when speaking to two warlords who were stopping the feeding stations.

When I came to Nairobi, to a big press conference, I wanted to tell the story. I felt overwhelmed by the sense of suffering and I felt a frustration that we weren't doing more to try to address the issue. That was what caused me to lose my composure.

I was furious because I was a trained barrister and I was supposed to be telling the world calmly, clearly and logically and my emotions were coming to the surface. I felt very disappointed with myself afterwards.

I went up to the hotel room, Nick [her husband] was consoling me and saying it was ok; and then the TV was on and I suddenly realized that it was much more compelling.

(Extract from BBC Radio 4 *Desert Island Discs*, 28 July 2013 Robinson, 2013a.)

Pacing change

Change requires high levels of energy and stamina as well as persistence. Not many of us, if we're honest, find it easy to do things differently. Sometimes that's because change is imposed. Sometimes we don't agree with the change (and maybe rightly), but more often it's just hard to adjust our thinking patterns and habits. It's even harder as we get older because we see the world through the lens of our own feelings, experiences, insecurities and achievements.

Pacing change to move at the right speed is helped by regularly taking the temperature of the whole stakeholder group: pausing frequently to check what stakeholders think and feel, want and need, and integrating this with factual data before taking decisions. Truly respecting that people need to be ready before they can adapt to change (except in emergencies) is critical to successful delivery, mainly because it motivates leaders to put effort into creating the conditions to help stakeholders move forward – that is, they understand why change is needed, what impact it will have on them, and how they need to adjust to it.

Investing this time pays off. It helps you find out earlier the things you don't know. Those are the details that later may become the unwelcome and unintended consequences that derail many a project. Multi-dimensional and complex projects inherently carry greater risk. You can reduce risk by pacing change to allow time to evaluate the whole system and not just the immediate issue, and by checking that what you are doing is consistent with your strategic aims and values.

Pacing change

When Coca-Cola, competing with Pepsi, renamed its drink 'New Coca-Cola' to attract more customers, market share fell rapidly because consumers were not ready for a 'new' drink. When Coca-Cola changed the marketing campaign to 'The Real Thing', that resonated with customers and sales went up.

When the British Labour Party changed its brand to 'New Labour', it won the next three elections. Voters and many party members were ready to leave the past behind. The old image was one of internal conflict, unpopular policies and excessive influence by extreme groups. The brand change to 'New Labour' symbolized a change of direction and offered an alternative to voters. New Labour won with a huge majority in 1997.

Maintains focus and strength of purpose; brings rigour and discipline to measurement of results

Focus on strategy

Strategies often fail because leaders lose sight of their goals. Leaders know when they set out on a journey what they want to achieve. But as we discussed in Chapter 4, Futurity, the environment inevitably changes; leaders have to adapt their strategies to fit the new contexts. And, as we argued, they must do this without losing focus on their overall vision.

Maintaining focus is generally recognized as a private sector strength, particularly by those from business who have worked in partnership with government. It's also been successfully applied in those NGOs where business disciplines have been imported – like the Gates Foundation.

Focus on values

Values are fundamental to how we engage with both internal and external stakeholders. The balance is often to remain focused, hold onto your values and beliefs, while respecting those of others at the same time.

Success rests on clear strategic aims and values that attract others to work with us in mutually beneficial partnerships. Deviating from these because of short-term pressures is a sure-fire way of losing credibility. So if, for example, an organization's values include supporting sustainable development but under pressure to reduce costs it acts in a way that is damaging to the environment, it risks losing the trust of customers and credibility with other stakeholders.

Strength of purpose

Strength and objectivity are necessary when stakeholders behave unreasonably or renege on agreements. We need to judge whether it's in our best interests to adapt to their demands or to respond robustly. Judging how to respond is best done in a disassociated state, by analysis of facts and objective evaluation of the pros and cons of different approaches.

When trust is broken, we feel strong emotions (anger, betrayal) but in a partnership we have to look beyond how we feel, at least in the short term, and decide objectively how to respond, taking time to identify and evaluate all options and deciding which approach best fits achievement of the future vision.

We spoke in Chapter 6 about empathy with the joint project and the importance of maintaining focus on the mission. These are moments when that empathy is tested. We have to judge how important the stakeholders are to the long-term strategy. For example, a business that has invested significantly in a joint venture with a government may have no choice but to work with it for some time to come. Then the business has to decide whether to respond robustly or accept 'realpolitik'. Non-profits face similar challenges, particularly in conflict zones.

Behaving robustly can involve making strong representations. But it might also mean utilizing creative thinking to change the game and do something your opponent is not expecting that puts you in a stronger position. Chess players will be familiar with the idea.

These game changers involve risk. Leaders need to be flexible, first strengthening their position and then making sure that their opponents do not lose face, particularly if they are important stakeholders who must be onside to deliver long-term aims. In Chapter 6 – Empathy with purpose – we touched on cultural competence. This understanding plays into judging the right move for the context and for the cultural environment.

Rigour

> It's a funny thing, the more I practise the luckier I get.
> (Arnold Palmer, world-class US golfer)

Success is sometimes attributed to luck. But while luck is a factor in life, more often success is the result of hard work and a rigorous approach. In this section we consider how rigour is part of versatility.

We looked at the importance of a systematic approach when identifying and managing stakeholders. This rigorous approach is necessary when dealing with immediate crises and preventing slow-burning problems turning into crises. Too often when dealing with change, decisions are based on poor-quality cost estimation, anticipated benefits that never realize, and solutions that are no longer relevant by the time they are implemented.

Why do these things happen? The common cause is lack of rigour, which plays out in the following ways:

- not allowing sufficient time to identify the facts;
- searching for facts to support existing thinking rather than objective evaluation;
- maintaining existing structures even though the situation has changed and new approaches are needed; and
- not establishing the legal and regulatory requirements in advance.

Rigour does not mean having all the answers. Jeff Raikes (2013) of the Gates Foundation offers this advice to his employees:

[Rigour means] engaging others in your sometimes messy thought processes. The focus needs to be analysing and challenging big ideas, not what facts you have memorized. We can't avoid difficult conversations because our work is hard and complex. We have to welcome regular intellectual dialogue with each other and our partners.

Measurement

Strategies often fail because leaders don't know whether what they are doing is achieving results. They have no way of measuring it. Generally governments are poorer at measurement, partly because the nature of their work makes identification of targets and measures less straightforward, and they often do not have the management information necessary to measure performance. One of the advantages of working in partnership with business, for government, is the discipline and rigour that business brings to measuring results.

Story: Measuring progress

Bill Gates talks about the importance of measurement in the context of non-profit and government partnerships.

I have been struck again and again by how important measurement is to improving the human condition. You can achieve amazing progress if you set a clear goal and find a measure that will drive progress toward that goal.

Given how tight budgets are around the world, governments are rightfully demanding effectiveness in the programs they pay for. To address these demands, we need better measurement tools to determine which approaches work and which do not.

I think the best example of picking an important goal and using measurement to achieve it is the vaccination work UNICEF did under Jim Grant's leadership in the 1980s. Few people may have heard of Grant, but his impact on the world was as significant as any profit-driven leader like a Henry Ford or Thomas Watson.

Grant set an ambitious goal of getting lifesaving vaccines out to 80 per cent of children worldwide. This wasn't easy in poor countries at a time when the fax machine was the most advanced communication tool. But once Grant put a robust data-gathering system in place, he was able to drive change. He could see which countries were successful in increasing their vaccination coverage rates and used that data to help other countries to do the same. The countries that were falling behind were embarrassed, and they focused more resources and attention on the problem than they would have without the data. Thanks to Grant's efforts and thousands of vaccinators, the percentage of infants worldwide receiving necessary vaccines rose from 17 per cent in 1980 to 75 per cent in 1990, saving millions of lives every year.

(Extracts from The Gates Foundation Annual Letter for 2013 (Gates, 2013).)

Exudes confidence, at ease and in touch with others' needs

A gymnast makes it look easy when performing in competition. Movements flow and the outward impression is one of grace and control. Internally the gymnast is fully stretched and the application is immense.

Understand the role and play it well

PQ leaders understand the importance of image, symbolism and behaviour. Mark Sedwill, based on his time in Afghanistan, observed that: 'it's important to play the role. *There is an element of theatre and it matters. Image is powerful.*'

Mark offered an example: he and the NATO force commanders (General McChrystal and General Petraeus) rarely wore body armour when visiting different parts of Afghanistan. Mark says, for him, 'it was a calculated decision. My job was to project confidence in the mission. The media were present and we were on camera a lot. And when we talked to local people in the markets they had no body armour. We needed to communicate confidence.'

Mark was at pains to point out that this was not about courage; they were well protected and did not allow serving officials or military to take unnecessary risks. But the symbolism was important.

In a different setting, Mary Robinson explained how she consciously changed her image when she was elected as the first woman President in Ireland. When the votes were first counted, she came second and only gained victory after votes from the third candidate were transferred across to her. However, during her time in office, she increased her approval ratings to 90 per cent and kept them there (Edemariam, 2010).

How did she do this? She claims she made herself less private and austere, acquiring suits by Irish designers, trying above all to be more open and approachable and more like her own gregarious mother. She reflected in an interview on Irish TV with Gay Byrne: 'The more I did that, the more I got back an extraordinary response.'

Playing it well in a crisis

Perhaps the most important time to play your role well is during a crisis. Here are some tips for handling that.

Top tips for playing it well in a crisis

However uncomfortable or under pressure you might feel in a crisis, when you engage with stakeholders you must project a strong sense that you are confident, calm and in control of both yourself and the situation. If you appear rattled, their confidence in you drops and your power to influence is diminished.

Perhaps the most important time to play your role well is during a crisis. Here are some tips for handling that.

Appearance

How do you look? Make sure that the basic things are in place and you are appropriately dressed to fit the situation and the environment. First impressions are visual. Even if you feel frazzled, you don't want to look it. You want to signal that you are coping well and are in control. So while dress may seem trivial in a crisis, it is not, because people initially judge you on your outward appearance.

Communication

What is your core message? Be clear about the 1–3 important things you must say. Practise in advance and make sure you can support your points if challenged. Credibility is lost if you falter under questioning.

How do you ensure that your message is heard? This goes back to the behaviour we talked about in Chapter 5, Power. To be memorable, the message needs to be simple but not simplistic. Use tools like metaphor or narrative. Paint a picture for listeners.

Slow down: create space in your communication. Allow pauses. Change the flow of your speech so that speaking quicker is punctuated with speaking a little slower to add emphasis and rhythm.

Stay grounded: remember who you are and what you have to offer. Keep connected to your own integrity and values. They'll shine through when you speak to others and make your message more compelling.

Be still: stillness projects calmness, control and a natural authority. Others will then have confidence in you.

Take a moment to learn from the people you have observed who appear ill at ease. You might notice some common characteristics to avoid. Here are a few:

- defensive;
- placating;
- deferential;
- aggressive;
- needing approbation;

- saying too much or too little;
- shallow breathing;
- not maintaining eye contact.

Personal confidence

PQ leaders who are confident in their own abilities inspire confidence in others. Here are some of their common characteristics that you might find it helpful to remember:

- courteous, but not deferential;
- say what is necessary with energy, pace and concision, but no rush;
- avoid self-justification;
- defend the points that matter;
- not seeking validation or praise;
- not knocked off balance by criticism.

Of course in reality we may be feeling anything but confident. Sir Richard Branson, who is known for taking risks in both business and his personal life, confesses that he can feel extremely nervous on occasions. Sheryl Sandberg, COO of Facebook, offers the following advice (in her influential book *Lean In*, 2013): 'When I don't feel confident, one tactic I've learned is that it sometimes helps to fake it.'

There is plenty of research that makes the link between thought and behaviour. If you think it, you do it. If you do it enough, you believe it. The literature on the power of positive thinking argues the case for optimism persuasively.

The key takeaway is that if you change your mind-set, even by 'faking it', it can help you change your behaviour. And, if you change the way you behave, you change how others feel about you.

Ease

Perhaps the hallmark of the leaders who exude political intelligence is their personal ease. They all have a powerful presence, but whether their influence comes from business, politics or religion, they know what matters to them and they're at ease with themselves. They are not trying to prove anything. This frees them up to be curious, challenging, gracious and remarkably lacking in personal ego. There is nothing grand about them, but they are compelling.

Jeff Bewkes remarked that the people who have a reputation for being good at managing upwards rarely make good top leaders when they become the boss. 'I tell them, you're in the right position now, you're playing to your strengths. Don't move up.'

And while PQ leaders do hold people accountable for their actions, they understand that things will go wrong despite the best efforts of all stakeholders. And that they have to be ready to forgive and move on. Gandhi memorably said: 'The weak never forgive. Forgiveness is an attribute of the strong.'

Recognizes political reality; knows when to push and when to concede; and works with the politics to achieve objectives

> You need to have very good political antennae and know when the wind is changing.
>
> (Dame Denise Holt, non-executive director, HSBC Bank plc)

There will be times when, however strongly you believe in something or however important it is to your strategic objectives, the timing isn't right and it's not possible to exercise influence. Public opinion might be too strong or the political imperative too great. Versatile leaders know when to persist and when to concede. It's a delicate judgement. Both require courage and vision.

Persisting

Persisting with something that appears a lost cause because it's fundamental to achieving your objectives can lead to criticism. It's hard to bring joint stakeholders and partners with you, particularly over the long term.

British Prime Minister Margaret Thatcher found persistence paid off early in her term of office when she led reform of industrial relations. She had high levels of political support and had timed her intervention to ensure she had the resources to take on the National Union of Mineworkers. Later on, her persistence with the poll-tax was one factor in her downfall because she no longer had the same level of political support among her colleagues or the country.

Persistence can build trust. When a leader takes a position and persists with it even when that is not to their advantage, it can build trust and respect because people know what he/she stands for.

Judgement is needed to assess the right time to push forward. How you form that judgement is based on understanding the politics of the situation and thinking ahead to identify what factors might lead to a change in attitudes in your favour and a readiness to act when the moment comes.

NGOs are often in the difficult position of trying to persist with their humanitarian efforts in conflict situations. They have to balance the help they are offering the vulnerable with the risk to their own personnel. Each situation is judged on its merits, taking account of the best information available and consulting all stakeholders. In these circumstances, leaders take decisions by weighing up the lesser of evils and understanding the risks and consequences of their actions.

Conceding

Conceding is hard. It can mean writing off costs and admitting to being wrong. Stakeholders may feel uncomfortable. But it's worth remembering that it is the most innovative – and therefore in the long term the most successful – leaders who try new approaches, and inevitably some will fail.

Failure to concede to forces that you can't control leads to crisis. The politically astute bail out earlier. The Starbucks example is a telling one. There were three global companies (Starbucks, Amazon and Google) who were identified as avoiding paying UK corporation tax. But only Starbucks had to concede, because their customers could easily buy their coffee elsewhere. It was the combination of behaving in a way that customers objected to, the ease with which customers could switch to another supplier and pressure from their franchisees that meant concession was the only option.

Here is some good advice for business when working with government.

Top tips

- It's important, if you are a smaller company, to remember that government does not owe you anything. It is not scared of you and it is not attracting you in. Therefore think of something to tell ministers that they don't know and which is useful to them.

- Companies need to recognize when there is such a political imperative that there is no point taking on government.

- In other situations there is scope to take on government, for example when a politician's position is not secure.

(Lord Kerr, then Deputy Chairman of Shell.)

To close this section, we offer examples of both persistence and concession.

Examples

Persisting

Bono recounted that when the Make Poverty History campaign first tried to influence the US Administration on tackling poverty in Africa, Paul O'Neill (adviser to President Bush) told him: 'if you think we are going to increase aid to Africa you are out of your mind' (Adams, 2008).

A few years later and after a lot of persuasion and joint work, $726 billion dollars of debt was cancelled.

Bob Geldof, talking to the *Guardian* newspaper about the influencing process on President George W Bush, commented that when politicians 'see the reality of policy on people, it startles them'.

Conceding

Starbucks in 2013 paid £20m in UK tax. Not because they were legally obliged too, nor because of UK Government or regulatory authorities' pressure. The leverage was UK customers choosing to buy their coffee elsewhere once Starbuck's tax avoidance strategies became known through organized campaigns on Twitter and other social media.

Conclusion

PQ leaders approach implementation of strategy and of building and maintaining relationships with focus and discipline. When they need to stand fast, they have the strength to do so. Even when the pressure is intense they do not buckle. Notwithstanding, they look systematically for opportunities to move forward and have the versatility to change tactics or adapt to new situations. They make these adaptations in a controlled way, knowing when to push and when to concede, and without losing focus on overall aims and values.

Personally they're at ease, understanding what is needed and having sufficient self-command to deliver it. They are not grand in their manner or self-promoting, but they are nonetheless compelling.

An African man who was for many years a political prisoner and went on to become a global leader, respected, admired and loved across the world, advised a group of the most eminent men and women when he set up the Elders: 'It's your task to listen very carefully: be humble. Don't go into a place thinking you know more than the people there' (Nelson Mandela).

PART THREE
How to develop PQ capability

Developing PQ as a leader

09

> *Let him who would move the world, move himself first.*
> **(SOCRATES)**

PQ leaders want to make a positive difference to the world. They achieve this through their determination, skill and capacity for learning. They mobilize people from across their networks to see and deliver a better future through shared leadership.

How to develop your PQ skills

First you have to believe there is a benefit to you in developing PQ. If you do, then you will need to invest time and effort into your development. PQ leadership is demanding and requires reflection and practice to achieve fluency.

Our key message to you is STOP! No one can develop PQ while running on a corporate treadmill.

If you are serious about developing PQ, we suggest that you use this chapter as a guide to support you through the early stages of your PQ development. We will recommend reading, courses and practical exercises to support you in building your capability.

The starting point is to consider how you learn best. You may know this, in which case you will know if reading is your preferred way of learning or whether shadowing someone works better for you. Most people never stop to think about how they learn best and have adapted to the dominant style of their tutors or seniors. You will do best if you approach your development of PQ through learning in a style that works best for you. To help you identify your preferred learning style you may want to consider a model for learning styles that was originally developed by Kolb and enhanced by Honey and Mumford. It describes the four key approaches to learning:

- *Reflector*: Prefers to learn from activities that allow them to watch, think and review what has happened. Likes to use journals and brainstorming. Lectures are helpful if they provide expert explanations and analysis.

- *Theorist*: Prefers to think problems through in a step-by-step manner. Likes lectures, analogies, systems, case studies, models and readings. Talking with experts is normally not helpful.

- *Pragmatist*: Prefers to apply new lessons to actual practice to see if they work. Likes laboratories, field work and observations. Likes feedback, coaching and obvious links between the task-on-hand and a problem.

- *Activist*: Prefers the challenges of new experiences, involvement with others, assimilation and role-playing. Likes anything new, problem solving and small group discussions.

We suggest that you design your own PQ development plan, tailored to fit the way you learn best. This will make it attractive to you and increase the odds for more success as you willingly invest time and energy into developing PQ leadership.

How will you know if you are making progress?

The danger with any behavioural change is an enthusiastic start followed by a lack of follow through. How are you going to ensure that you sustain your new ways of behaving and do not slip back into your old ways? We suggest that you talk to someone else about your plan and have regular conversations about your progress. By contracting with someone else to discuss your development you are more likely to feel a commitment to report progress and will also benefit from sharing your experience and receiving feedback. This support can be invaluable as new ways of thinking and relating become hard-wired.

Where do I start?

We know that PQ capability comes from the ability to use all five facets in harmony. However you need a good level of capability for each facet before you can harmonize them.

If you have data about how you perform against the indicators that support each of the facets, you may be able to identify your development needs. If you do not have this data then you can download a tool that you can use to collect (360 degree feedback) data on your performance against the facets from relevant stakeholders and colleagues. Details of the tool can be found at www.pqleadership.com. Using the tool will give you a robust basis for identifying your development needs, especially if it's used in conjunction with coaching.

If you already have data on your performance against the PQ facets, then you can use the simple process shown in Table 9.1 to map further development activity. To complete Column 2, look at the PQ indicators and list those that you have not developed or need to develop more. In Column 3, write down specifically how you plan to develop these aspects of your performance.

The five facets are explored in detail in Chapters 4 to 8. You may want to revisit specific chapters and align some of the ideas there to the suggestions that follow.

TABLE 9.1 PQ personal development plan

The 5 facets	What specifically would improve my capability?	Personal development action
Futurity		
Power		
Empathy		
Trust		
Versatility		

Developing PQ capability across the five PQ facets

Futurity

PQ leaders have minds that can travel through time, see connections and weave solutions to deliver a better future.

Futurity is only possible if you stop, step back and take the time to reflect on what is happening, what has happened in the past and what may be possible in the future.

Be curious, keep abreast of what is happening in the world

PQ leaders are future-focused, constantly scanning the horizon for new possibilities. Their interest in global affairs keeps them and their organizations open to new ways of thinking and working. They are curious to meet people who work in completely different organizations. They listen, reflect and ask probing questions because they are genuinely interested in understanding. They are generous with their time, as they know that by engaging in conversations about the future of society, business and government can create ways of working together for the benefit of everyone. Individuals who work like this are often described by others as visionary. This may sound like a rare talent but, like most capabilities, when analysed many of the skills can be developed.

Envision a better future

Futurists are able to disassociate, to reflect, to dream and to free themselves to think of a future way beyond the constraints of the current reality. The frenetic pace of work and the lack of time available for reflection tend to encourage leaders to shoot straight to planning and to bypass or minimize the time for visioning. We know there is a huge expectation for leaders to deliver instant solutions and to be seen to be doing something. It takes time to explore what you and others want for the future; there are no shortcuts.

There are lots of books you can read about building a vision. Some of the best are to be found in the business psychology section.

Learning bite

- Keep up to date with political and business news – national and international. Use a range of media to get different perspectives.

- Talk about the news.

- Raise conversations with colleagues and friends that are far reaching: 'What if…'

- Actively seek out people who work in different organizations. Meet for coffee, lunch…

- Attend conferences and training programmes that have participants from a wide range of backgrounds and sectors.

- Stay curious, open and non-judgemental.

One book that appeals to people with a preference for structure is *The Solutions Focus* by Jackson and McKergow. It introduces a model with clear stages to support individuals and teams in creating a compelling vision for the future. Having envisioned what Jackson and McKergow call 'the future perfect', realistic stages are identified and agreed, with specific actions to achieve progress towards the future perfect. The process includes a numerical scale for reviewing progress.

For those who prefer a less structured approach, the Disney Creativity Strategy may appeal (see box overleaf). The Disney Creativity Strategy was developed by Robert Dilts, a pioneer in neuro-linguistic programming (NLP). He was interested to understand how Disney has maintained its success over time; Walt Disney had the ability to connect vision to business delivery. The success of the brand was based on this; Walt Disney was a futurist. By working with the Disney organization Dilts was able to identify that one of the reasons for Disney's success is the ability to see the future from different perspectives, which he described as three rooms.

All of us have a preferred room. If you are working on your own, be aware of your own natural preference and blind spots and take the time to think in the other two rooms so as to increase the robustness of your strategy. A fun way for a team to use the strategy is for those with a natural preference for each room to lead the process in that room and to stop people from limiting possibilities or rushing ahead to the next room.

The Disney Creativity Strategy

1 The Dream room: Dream and dream until you can dream no more. No buts or maybes, no limitations.

2 The Strategy room: The room where realists ask how close to the dream can you get at this moment in time. Have we got the resources? How long will it take? What is the strategy to achieve the vision?

3 The Critics' room: The strategy is evaluated by critics who challenge and improve it. Critics can critique the strategy but never the dream, as that would stop the dreamers dreaming.

Creating a vision that works for everyone in the golden triangle is complex. It is critical to engage with all stakeholders at the vision stage. Working collectively to develop a vision helps to build commitment and collective ownership and increases the likelihood of success.

Learning bite

- Take the time to dream.

- Share your dreams and encourage others to dream/vision a better future.

- Be curious and open to new ways of thinking about the world. Ask questions and listen to others.

- Read books on visioning, eg *The Dream Society* by Rolf Jensen.

- Practise visioning techniques, eg The solutions focus – OSKAR model, the Disney Creativity Strategy.

- Go on a short course on neuro-linguistic programming. NLP has lots of frameworks for visioning a better future.

If you are confident of your ability to vision but less confident about translating a vision into a strategy, then a strategy programme may help. Strategy programmes will introduce you to a wide range of strategy frameworks, from which you can select those that resonate most with your context. They can help you to raise your awareness about the possibilities and the potential barriers to success. Frameworks bring structure to the strategic process and provide a common language, enabling people to understand each other. Be selective about the programme you choose, as too many strategy programmes jump straight to the strategy and planning stage and rarely explore in depth the power of visioning. The danger of strategy without vision is that it will not stretch your thinking to deliver the ambitious futures demanded in a shared power world.

Learning bite

- Embed thinking about the future into your business schedule.

- Help others to be future-focused by including visioning and strategic planning at your meetings.

- Do regular strategy reviews to check you are on track. Do you need to 're-set' the strategy in response to any changes in the environment?

- *The Strategy Book* by Max McKeown is good on vision and strategy implementation.

- Seek out people and companies that can support you and your organization to be more future-focused, eg the Mind Gym and ?What If!

- When was the last time that you suggested an innovative idea that was adopted? If it is more than six months ago – make time for thinking creatively either with colleagues or on your own depending on your preference and see if you can increase the frequency.

Some PQ leaders are natural futurists; however most develop capability from a range of experiences over time. For young leaders it is important to find opportunities to develop futurity early. Ask for secondments to shadow senior leaders who are recognized as visionary thinkers. This will give you insights as to how they do this and you can integrate some of their approaches in the way you work. Ask to attend board meetings and executive meetings as an observer, join policy groups or project teams, even serve as minutes secretary. The earlier in your career that you can get an overview as to how your organization works and how it relates to others, the easier it will be for you to understand how you can most effectively contribute to its future.

Power

PQ leaders understand power and carry their own power well. When developing this facet, it is easiest to separate power into these two parts and then bring them back together.

Learning bite

Identifying and engaging stakeholders

- Remember that power is fragmented. You need to think broadly about stakeholders. Hold a brainstorming session with colleagues and some stakeholders and work through the stakeholder questions in Chapter 5.

- Once you have identified your various stakeholder groups, use the influence/support matrix (in Chapter 5) to prioritize your efforts on engagement.

- Think broadly and creatively about how to engage the different groups. It is more likely that you will need to expand your current network of stakeholders to forge new relationships so as to meet the more complex and large-scale leadership challenges of a PQ world.

- To find out more about how government works and about influencing politicians and officials in the UK and internationally – read *Lobbying: The art of political persuasion* by Lionel Zetter.

Understanding power

In most organizations, surprisingly few people have real power or influence. Being clear about who has power in any specific context will provide focus as to who can makes things happen. For you to have power, you need to know these people and they need to know you. To secure access to these people, think about what motivates and interests them and why they might be interested in you. What do you know or can you do that will attract their attention? How can you be helpful to them in achieving their goals?

Personal power

Having identified the key stakeholders, how do you grab their attention? A great way to think about this is to use a model created by Michael Grinder and explored in his book *Charisma: The art of relationships*. He looks at two dimensions: power and relationships.

The first dimension describes how we carry our power. If we carry power well, we are at ease with ourselves; it is obvious from the way we relate and our body language that we are comfortable with power and do not need to badge ourselves or rely on positional power to be noticed and heard. If we carry power less well, our body language is closed and eye contact reduced as though we are making ourselves invisible. Our language also signals how much power we have; for example, starting a sentence with 'I am just...' sounds like an apology and any power we may have is thrown away in the opening line. How often do you hear a doctor say 'I am just a doctor'? We reveal much about how powerful we are through our body language and behaviour. People read all these signals, generally at an unconscious level, and will afford to us the power we afford ourselves.

Grinder's second dimension is about relationships and whether we are naturally interested and relate well to other people or not. Again people can read this in our behaviour. This dimension harmonizes with empathy with purpose and trust. The most powerful people carry their power well and are interested in and relate well to others.

You may have completed some psychometric instruments in the past. These may be worth re-reading as many of them will summarize your profile and provide guidance on how best to go about influencing people with different profiles. You may also have completed a 360° feedback report that captures how you see yourself compared with how others experience you. These reports generally capture feedback as scores, which is helpful, but many include narrative feed-back that can be even more revealing as to how we are perceived: eg 'he needs to work on his personal impact...'

Learning bite

Psychometrics

- If you have done psychometrics, re-read them and think about what they say about you and how best to influence others.

- Ask your HR director, head of learning and development or coach if you can do some psychometric tests that will help you to understand power and influence; these include the Strength Deployment Inventory (SDI), the Myers-Briggs Type Indicator (MBTI) and the Fundamentals of Interpersonal, Relations Orientation Behaviour (FIRO-B).

In Chapter 5, we explored story and metaphor as tools of the most powerful communicators. Can you communicate the future clearly, simply and inspire others to work with you? There are lots of books about leaders as storytellers, and no doubt many great leaders that you can think of who use story to get their message across in a compelling and memorable way. You need to be able to do this. How would a journalist get your message across? Be your own hack. Say out loud what you wrote, it helps to hear it rather than see it.

In our experience power is rarely discussed; the word is almost a cultural taboo. Power exists and PQ leaders understand how to use it to influence others in support of their projects and wider vision.

Learning bite

- Watch television and films, noting the most powerful communicators. Borrow some of their techniques and make them your own.

- Read books about storytelling and the power of story.

- Read biographies and autobiographies of people you admire as great storytellers.

- Think consciously about your body language, especially for the big set pieces. Make sure your body language is aligned to your message.

- Work with a coach, mentor or actor to explore and develop your personal impact.

- Bring energy and urgency to the way you communicate. Let people see that you have a passion and that you care. Turn up the lights, shine!

Empathy with purpose

The ability to 'walk in another person's shoes' and purposefully use this insight to deliver change for the benefit of humanity.

The stories in Chapter 6 illustrate how PQ leaders can do this in ways ranging from on a one-to-one basis through to large groups and organizations. Empathy with purpose operates at the level of feelings combined with intellect and the drive to deliver a better future.

Empathy with purpose is the alchemy of PQ, its heart and glue. It supports PQ leaders in harmonizing the five PQ facets. Empathy with purpose enables us to trust more rapidly, to envision a future that includes and appeals to all stakeholders in futurity, to know whether we should flex or stand strong. And finally, empathy with purpose helps us to understand power and how best to connect with it.

Empathy

Empathy is at the core of emotional intelligence (EQ). A good starting point is the book *Emotional Intelligence* by Daniel Goleman, the first writer to capture the importance of emotion as well as reasoning in determining success. The core proposition of EQ is that life success requires a combination of an average level of 'traditional intelligence' with an above-average level of 'emotional intelligence'. There are a wide range of psychometric tests available that measure EQ. These include self-score tests that are quick and easy (of limited use if you are not self-aware!) through to a selection of 360° assessment tools.

Think of the people with whom you have empathy. How do you know you have empathy? How was that relationship developed? What could you be doing more of or less of to achieve empathetic relationships with your key stakeholders. One CEO wanted to improve his ability to build rapport with people; when asked if he could recall a time when he was good at rapport he replied: 'When I fell in love.' When asked how, he replied: 'I was interested, I listened, I cared.' He knew how to build rapport, but he was not investing the time and attention to do so in a work context.

We are surrounded by opportunities on a daily basis to practise empathy with purpose. Start by becoming more aware of others and think about what they want, as well as what you want. Once you can do this, push yourself further by actively trying out their different perceptual positions (we covered this technique in some detail in Chapter 6). If you can develop the ability to view a situation from multiple perspectives, you are more likely to find ways of working that will engage and align you more closely with others. Try not to read all behaviour at a surface level; dig deeper and think about what may be motivating people's behaviour; for example, expressed anger could be frustration.

A senior director we knew was upsetting the board of his organization by behaving badly at meetings. He seemed obstructive, dismissing any ideas for the future. In light of his behaviour the board were considering his dismissal. When the director was asked directly why he was being so disruptive, he replied: 'I have worked for this company since I left university and I care about it. The proposed strategy will destroy this company.' He then went on to share his concerns, most of which made sense to the board. He told them why he thought the strategy was flawed and collectively they 're-set' the strategy, which secured the company's future.

Learning bite

- Thinking about other people, their situation, wants and dreams

- Be generous with your time, get to know people, actively listen, observe and ask probing questions.

- Be helpful to others, show concern, keep in touch.

- Go beyond immediately responding to someone's surface behaviour. Ask yourself what may be driving their behaviour. Learn to separate the person and the behaviour.

- Be forgiving; most people are doing their best.

- Think about those with whom you have empathy. How did you develop that empathy? What could you be doing more or less of to achieve empathy with others?

- Experiment with techniques like perceptual positions, to see how others see the world and how they may see you.

With purpose

Empathy with purpose is selective and focused towards achieving positive outcomes with a wide range of stakeholders. At work people are generally attracted to others based on the way they relate and behave. You need to be clear about your own beliefs, what matters to you and what you want from your work and life. These are big questions, deep questions. If you are unclear, then you will need to embark on an inner journey to find your purpose. People follow people that they believe in, which means you need to know what you believe first. Once you are clear, find roles that enable you to achieve your purpose and for which you have the skills and networks to mobilize and support you in making the world a better place for future generations.

Learning bite

- Leadership is an inner journey. What are your beliefs and values? Try writing a mission statement for yourself.

- Act in accordance with your beliefs and values.

- Respect the beliefs and values of others.

- What is your passion? Share your passion with others who want to positively improve our legacy to future generations.

- How could your organization change the way it operates to deliver more for society? Run an event to capture ideas from colleagues and stakeholders.

- How diverse and culturally aware is your organization? How could you open up thinking and identify new partners with different experiences?

Trust

PQ leaders are trusted. Trust is critical to achieving good working relationships. In a world of contracting, mergers and acquisitions, regulation, legal agreements and formal process, PQ leaders place a high importance on trust. Although often perceived as intangible, trust is what makes the difference in building lasting relationships. PQ leaders are highly selective about who they choose to trust. They know from experience that those they trust can be called upon for support and positive challenge.

Trust may seem an old-fashioned concept: 'My word is my bond.' However, even though some leaders struggle to define trust, they all know instinctively who they can trust. These are the people they choose to have around them, especially in a crisis.

Learning bite

Reading

- The *Ashridge Management Index,* which started in 1994, includes a survey of what followers most value in their leaders. Every year trust/integrity is rated Number 1.

- *Exemplary Leadership* by Kouzes and Posner identifies mutual trust as what sustains extraordinary efforts (2011).

- *The Speed of Trust: The one thing that changes everything,* by S Covey (2006).

- '*Building your company's vision*', HBR article by Collins and Porras (1996).

- The *Harris Reputational Index Poll* and the *Edelman Trust Barometer* to understand public perceptions of trust. Both are available online.

There may be others around with higher qualifications or more experience, but trust determines who is in the inner circle.

How can you build trust?

How do people assess who they can trust? What are those people doing that builds trust, garners support and enables them to lead with courage and conviction even when under extreme pressure?

Collins and Porras, in their classic *Harvard Business Review* (1999) article 'Building your company's vision', introduce the concept of a 'Mars Group'. Imagine that you had to recreate the very best attributes of your organization on another planet but you have only have seats for seven people on your rocket ship: who would you send? Generally people are surprised by how difficult it is to name seven people. Invariably the final seven are highly credible individuals who articulate their own and the organization's core values precisely because they are exemplars of those values – ie a representative slice of the organization's genetic code. The question to ask yourself is: If the rocket test was applied to your organization, would you be chosen as one of the seven people trusted to recreate the best of your organization? If not, why not? And therefore what do you need to start doing to be chosen?

To build trust people need to know who you are and what you stand for. Inevitably, young leaders spend much of their early career conforming to the culture of their organization and keeping those above them happy, and rarely consciously think about their own leadership profile. Senior leaders have to be able to connect and communicate in a way that captures who they are and what they stand for. People have to know you, to trust you. People want to know what you believe, your values, how you like to work, what they can expect from you and what you expect of them. To be a leader you need followers, and followers are increasingly demanding and selective about whom they will follow. Technical brilliance alone is not enough; people want to know who you are and what you stand for.

Valerie runs programmes on leadership branding and personal impact. She introduces branding by asking participants to name the brands they trust and why. Having understood the process of branding, we ask them to think about the brands of individual leaders and to work out their leadership brand essence. Having worked on branding others, we ask them to consider their own leadership brand and whether it truly captures their essence. To be successful, your brand needs to be honest, clear and capture the best of you.

What are your attributes, what are the benefits of these and finally if you had to capture your leadership brand in three words, what would you choose? This is what differentiates you from other leaders. PQ leaders are trusted because they are clear about who they are and what they stand for.

Once you have worked on your draft brand, ask others how they would capture your leadership brand in three words. Ask those who know you well and include some new contacts to get their first impressions. Do any of the words they choose match the ones you chose? If they do, then your self-awareness is high and your brand is clear. If not, it may be because they value things about you, that you take for granted, or that you have underestimated or overestimated your brand. Just by doing this exercise, you will be signalling that you are open to feedback and willing to engage with others to improve your performance, which will help to build trust.

Learning bite

Leadership branding – to elicit your leadership brand ask yourself:

- What are people saying about you? How do they describe you?

- How would you like to be perceived?

- Is your brand a clear manifestation of what you stand for?

- Does your behaviour make it easy for people to work out your brand?

- Does what you believe, say and do stack up. Are you and your brand aligned?

- Can you be trusted to deliver this brand consistently?

We all have a leadership brand, whether we attend to it or not. Many leaders are not clear about what they stand for and therefore, not surprisingly, people have unclear and mixed perceptions of them.

Track record

We know that a good track record of delivering what you say you will deliver builds trust. What is your track record? Can people rely on you? If not, then start building a track record. Time will tell if you can be trusted to consistently deliver. Build a reputation for delivering joint endeavours. Once you develop this track record, people will talk about you as someone who can be trusted and increase the likelihood of others seeking you out for partnership working.

In brief, your behaviour and track record will determine whether people trust you. Anything less than this will leave people unsure about you. Think about the people you trust: what is it specifically about them that you trust? And what might you be doing more of or less of to enable people to have greater trust in you?

Long-term projects that benefit society

- Find out about the B Team (www.bteam.org) and keep in touch with their research, activities and thinking.
- Learn about the work the Elders (www.theelders.org) are doing to help resolve conflict.
- Follow companies online that are pursuing the sustainability agenda, and be inspired about new ways to help society and make a profit. Read *People, Planet, Profit* by Peter Fisk (2010) pp 204–210.
- Choose suppliers that show commitment to society, and start to build your reputation for caring about society.

Versatility

PQ leaders can flex both analytically and behaviourally in pursuit of their goals. This provides choice and choice increases their potential impact.

Analytical

PQ leaders have vision and will stand strong or flex to keep on track as they confront the reality of delivery. Recognizing the value of anticipation, they scan the environment to identify changes ahead of time and to avert crises.

To stay ahead of the game you need to constantly scan for change in the environment and remain close to all the key players. The context and the politics may change and you have to know when to push and when to concede to achieve your objectives.

Learning bite

- What scanning and monitoring systems do you have in place?
- How robust are they?
- Do you discuss with colleagues potential scenarios and how you might respond to them?
- How do you ensure that you are innovative and ahead of the trend?
- Read Clayton Christenson's *The Innovator's Dilemma*.

Behavioural

As the leader and as one of the most powerful people in the organization, you have to be in command of your behaviour and able to respond with versatility to the demands of the situation and the people around you.

Our individual way of leading is shaped by our past, our present and our psychological preferences. You need to be aware of your own preferences and yet be open to expanding the range of behaviours available to you.

By raising your self-awareness and practising new ways of behaving you will increase your behavioural range and fluency. By assessing, calibrating and moving with ease across a range of behaviours you will be able to connect more readily with people from across a wider range of organizations and cultures. In Chapter 8 we used the metaphor of a gymnast to capture the essence of versatility: strength and flexibility, which are achieved through practice and by acquiring muscle memory. So it is with behavioural versatility: the more we practise, the greater likelihood we have of saying and doing the right thing in the moment.

Learning bite

Psychometrics

The psychometric instruments we mentioned earlier may help to raise your self-awareness. Another instrument worth exploring is *Situational Leadership* by Hersey and Blanchard. It considers the balance of directive and supportive behaviour in your leadership style and how you can flex your behaviour across four styles to effectively engage, lead and develop other people. The research supporting this instrument found that only 1 per cent of all leaders use all four styles available to them, 10 per cent use three, 35 per cent use two and 54 per cent of leaders use only one style. It seems that even though we know we need to be versatile, in practice, and especially under pressure, we stick to type.

The Strength Deployment Inventory (SDI) by Elias H Porter considers your strengths in relating to others when everything is going well and when you are faced with conflict and opposition.

Learning bite

- Think of leaders you know who remain consistent in their beliefs and yet can seamlessly shift their style to engage a wide range of people. Observe them closely and try to integrate some of their behaviours into your own leadership style.

- Seek feedback to understand how you might improve your performance. Ask your boss, peers, direct reports and key stakeholders for feedback: eg How am I doing? What do you appreciate? What specifically could I be doing more of or less of that would be helpful? People are generally flattered to be asked and you are role-modelling being open to learning.

There will be times when conversations are difficult, there is conflict, and moving beyond the current obstacles may seem impossible. The book *Fierce Conversations* by Susan Scott is based on the belief that our lives succeed or fail one conversation at a time. You may also want to identify and understand your own preference for dealing with conflict. The Thomas–Kilmann Conflict Mode Instrument (TKI) is a self-scoring assessment that provides interpretation and feedback on your personal preference and explores in which scenarios competing, collaborating, compromising, avoiding or accommodating would be the most effective position.

Learning bite

When the going gets tough!

- How confident and skilled are you at robust conversations?

- Complete and study the Thomas–Kilmann Conflict Mode Instrument (TKI).

- Read *Fierce Conversations* by Susan Scott.

Self-command, understanding how to associate and disassociate, and managing your personal presence are arts that the best leaders learn. You can learn from books, observation and training. But the best learning comes from experience and reflection on that experience that leads to change and improvement.

Learning bite

- Association and disassociation is covered in NLP literature. See the earlier references to Robert Dilts and neuro-linguistic programming.

- Mindfulness helps leaders manage their emotions. A good starter book is authored by Mark Williams and Danny Penman.

- Train with professional actors to become more aware of the different tones and movements that you can use to signal your mood and feelings or to conceal them.

Developing PQ in your organization

10

> *"An organization's ability to learn, and translate that learning into action rapidly, is the ultimate competitive advantage.* (JACK WELCH, FORMER CHAIRMAN AND CEO OF GENERAL ELECTRIC)

Overview

This chapter offers guidance on how to develop PQ across your organization and tools to help with implementation. Section 1 describes how to assess skills levels. Section 2 offers options for integrating PQ into existing HR systems such as selection (recruitment and internal promotion), learning and development, competence frameworks and performance management.

PQ is a good-news story. It offers an opportunity to motivate and inspire employees and to re-energize collaborative efforts. As you work with your colleagues to interpret and apply it in your organization, make the most of the opportunity it offers to reinvigorate the way people feel and think about their work.

Before getting into the process, take the time to explain the addition of PQ to your leadership skills-set. Talking of processes like skills audits and training needs analysis may make employees feel threatened if it's not put into context.

To help you start a conversation about PQ with your colleagues, we've designed a short questionnaire to help people think about their organization's needs in a shared power world. The tool is in the Annex at the end of this chapter.

PQ skills audit

A first step to understanding the existing levels of PQ capacity in your organization is to conduct a skills audit. The aim is to find out:

- Which roles need PQ?
- What is the skill level of the people in those roles?
- What are their development needs?

To help you do this we've designed a simple skills audit model that involves:

- assessing the level of PQ needed in each leadership role;
- establishing where skills exist by role and function and where the gaps are located; and
- creating the data to inform development planning and budget decisions.

We've designed tools for two core groups:

- Group A is businesses, non-profits and international organizations that operate a business model.
- Group B is government, non-profits and international organizations that work more closely to the government model.

Identifying PQ roles

Every organization is different. The best approach is the one that fits your organizational needs. We've offered one approach below. You can tailor it to fit your own cultural and operational requirements.

Group A

Process: Set up a sub-group of the main board to oversee the implementation of PQ. Group members should include the CEO and/or the COO, working with the HR director, some members of the executive team, and the head of corporate communications.

Role: The first job is to assess PQ relevance to each role. This involves considering each role against defined criteria and making a judgement about whether PQ has high, medium or low relevance to successful completion of the role. A tool for doing this is shown in Table 10.1. Assessments should be entered in Column 1.

TABLE 10.1 Group A skill assessment tool

Function	How relevant is PQ to the role? Rate: H/M/L	Track record: Experience Rate: H/M/L	Track record: Delivery Rate: H/M/L
CEO			
Executive board			
Divisional CEOs home			
Divisional CEOs overseas			
Heads of departments/ operational units			
Team leaders			
High potential employees			

Once you know which roles have high or medium PQ relevance, it's the role of senior line managers to review the performance of individuals in those roles and assess their skill level based on their track record. The criteria for making an assessment are shown in Table 10.2. Results can be added to the table in Table 10.1 in Columns 2 and 3.

TABLE 10.2 Group A assessment criteria

Classification	High	Medium	Low
Experience	• Has led 3 or more complex projects involving multi-sector and multi-cultural stakeholders. • International experience.	Has led 1–3 complex projects involving either multi-sector or multi-cultural stakeholders.	Limited experience of leading complex projects but without multi-stakeholder involvement.
Delivery	• Successful delivery of projects. • Provided long-term value to the business. • Societal benefits identified, measured and delivered. • Reputation of business measurably enhanced with stakeholders and wider public.	• Successful delivery of projects. • Some medium and long-term value to the business – some opportunities missed. • Limited benefits to society. • Reputation not enhanced.	• Failed to deliver projects. • Short-term focus. • No benefit, or some detriment to society. • Reputation deteriorated.

Group B: Government/international organizations closely aligned with public sector models

Process: Set up a sub-group of the departmental/organizational main board to oversee implementation of PQ. The group members include the head of government department/international organization and/ or the COO, working with the HR director, some members of the executive team and the head of corporate communications.

Role: The first job is to assess the relevance of PQ to each role. This involves considering each role against defined criteria and making a judgement about whether PQ has high, medium or low relevance to the successful execution of the job. A tool for doing this is shown in Table 10.3 on the next page. Assessments should be entered in Column 1.

Once you know the level of PQ relevance for each role, it's the role of senior line managers to review the performance of individuals in those roles and assess skill levels based on their track record. The criteria for making an assessment are at Table 10.4 on page 221. Results should/can be added to the table in Table 10.3 in Columns 2 and 3.

Next steps

The second job for the sub-group is to review the final data set. Does it make sense? Does it pass the common-sense test? Any potential anomalies should be resolved at this point. Once there is sub-group agreement on the data, the next stage is to decide how to develop the individuals concerned.

To help you start, we've set out in Table 10.5 on page 222 some suggestions on appropriate development support for those individuals in roles with high or medium PQ relevance.

TABLE 10.3 Group B skill assessment tool

Function	How relevant is PQ to the role? *Rate: H/M/L*	Track record: Experience *Rate: H/M/L*	Track record: Delivery *Rate: H/M/L*
Ministers			
Heads of government departments			
Executive board members			
Directors Home			
Directors overseas			
Heads of departments/teams			
Deputy heads of departments			
Team leaders			
High potential employees			

TABLE 10.4 Group B assessment criteria

Classification	High	Medium	Low
Experience	• Has led 3 or more complex policy or service delivery projects involving multi-sector and multi-cultural stakeholders. • International experience.	• Has led 1–3 complex policy or service delivery projects involving either multi-sector or multi-cultural stakeholders.	• Limited experience of leading complex policy or service delivery projects. • Limited stakeholder involvement.
Delivery	• Successful delivery of projects. • Business and/or non-profit stakeholders achieved their agreed goals. • Long-term societal benefits identified, measured and delivered. • Reputation of government/ organization measurably enhanced with stakeholders and wider public.	• Successful delivery of projects. • Business and/or non-profit stakeholders achieved some of their agreed goals. • Medium-term societal benefits achieved but some opportunities missed to deliver value. • Reputation not damaged but not enhanced.	• Failed to deliver projects. • Short-term benefit for government/organization. • No benefit, or some detriment to society. • Reputation of government/ organization deteriorated.

TABLE 10.5 A diagnostic tool for PQ development

Track record: Experience Rate: H/M/L	Track record: Delivery Rate: H/M/L	Development required
H	H	• No development required. (Job holder is a potential mentor for others.)
H	M	• Tailored PQ coaching.
H	L	• Tailored PQ coaching. • Assign a senior mentor with high-level track record of delivery.
M	H	• Assign specific project to gain more experience. • Support with a mentor who has a high-level track record of delivery.
M	M	• PQ training programme to deepen understanding and develop skills. • Follow on coaching and mentoring during next assignment.
M	L	• PQ training programme to deepen understanding and develop skills. • Supervised assignment to put learning into action, supported by internal supervision. • Re-assess ratings after supervised assignment.
L	M	• PQ training programme to deepen understanding and develop skills. • Assign project to gain experience supported by a senior mentor with high-level record of delivery. • Offer tailored coaching.
L	L	• PQ training to deepen understanding and develop skills. • Assign a project to put learning into action supported by internal supervision. • Re-assess rating after supervised assignment.

FIGURE 10.1 Strategic HR Integration

Integrating PQ with other HR systems

Integrated HR systems help organizations to work better. Why? Because aligned processes mean that overall messages on culture, values, behaviours and skills are coherent and continually reinforced as people interact with the various HR systems.

When everyone has a shared understanding of what the organization wants and values, that informs how they do their jobs, how they manage their teams, how they relate to customers and stakeholders and to each other. When you add PQ, it clarifies how your people relate to wider society. It is the basis for explaining to everyone 'how' they should do their job – not the processes but the values and behaviours.

The model above (Figure 10.1) shows how the high-level HR processes fit. We'll explore each one in turn.

Competency frameworks

Many organizations have competency frameworks. Those that work effectively underpin other HR systems and are embedded and understood by the people who work in that organization.

Embedding PQ effectively requires communicating PQ behaviours to the organization but most importantly to those who occupy roles that have high or medium PQ relevance identified in the skills audits.

We recognize that every organization will need a slightly different approach. So here are some ideas on how to integrate PQ (Table 10.6 below). You can tailor them to fit your circumstances.

TABLE 10.6   How to adapt competency frameworks to fit PQ

Relevance of PQ to the role	Alignment between existing competency framework and PQ	Options for integrating PQ
High	75+% alignment with PQ indicators.	1 Refresh framework to increase %. 2 Provide additional guidance on PQ to those in high and medium-level PQ roles.
High/medium	Less than 75% alignment with PQ indicators.	1 Refresh existing framework to bring up to 90+%. 2 Write a role-specific PQ framework for those in high and medium-level PQ roles.
High/medium	No competency framework at this level.	1 Introduce PQ framework.
Low	Competencies exist.	1 Add indicator on awareness of PQ to framework. 2 Include awareness training element in induction and training programmes.

Learning and development

We recommend that five aspects of learning and development are reviewed as part of the implementation of PQ:

- coaching;
- formal training programmes;
- online learning;
- mentoring;
- assignments/secondments.

Formal training programmes

Part of the programme for introducing PQ should include review of your formal training offer to align it with the PQ facets and indicators. The level of redesign will be dictated by how important PQ is to the role. Where PQ relevance is low, some basic awareness training will meet the need. High or medium relevance roles need more.

More senior programmes will need significant re-design to integrate PQ into tutor-led sessions and experiential learning exercises.

Inviting external speakers with PQ skills from other sectors to contribute to your leadership programmes will give participants a broader view of how PQ is applied in different spheres.

Invite partners and organizations in other sectors to nominate participants to join your leadership programmes. By learning together, participants will build networks and create more opportunities for PQ working.

Overleaf is an example of how Rio Tinto approaches educating its senior managers about stakeholder engagement. Interestingly, in this case the formal training is sponsored by its Global Affairs Team, which spotted the PQ trend early.

Example: How Rio Tinto educates leaders in stakeholder engagement

When Rio Tinto realized it had a lot to learn about stakeholder engagement it developed, with the support of the McDonough School of Business at Georgetown University, a four-day programme in stakeholder engagement.

The Stakeholder Engagement Academy is a key part of a group-wide initiative to professionalize stakeholder engagement across Rio Tinto. The purpose is to maintain and enhance Rio Tinto's licence to operate and in turn support future growth.

Stakeholder engagement is critical to Rio Tinto. Robert Court, Global Head of External Affairs, and Judy Brown, Head of Stakeholder Engagement, recognize that stakeholders hold extraordinary power. Not only can they thwart progress, but they can threaten to halt a multibillion-dollar project already years under way. In Rio Tinto's experience, Judy Brown says: 'The success or failure of a project hinges more on stakeholder engagement than technical issues.'

The Rio Tinto programme is based on eight competencies and is based around tailored scenarios, which include role-play.

The programme is interactive and rooted in real situations. Feedback is positive – for example: 'It was good to try and put yourself in the shoes of a stakeholder with whom you normally engage' and 'The perception of what you think you would say in a situation is very different from what you actually say in role-playing.'

Three hundred executives completed the programme in 2012. Judy Brown, Rio Tinto's chief adviser for stakeholder management, is planning to deliver more programmes 'in country' and to broaden participation beyond executives.

Robert Court acknowledges that, even after an entire career of engaging with stakeholders, it remains difficult to pay attention to things often taken for granted, including the reflection of one's own bias and experience. 'It's a reminder of how diverse and dynamic the world is.'

FIGURE 10.2 Rio Tinto stakeholder engagement competencies

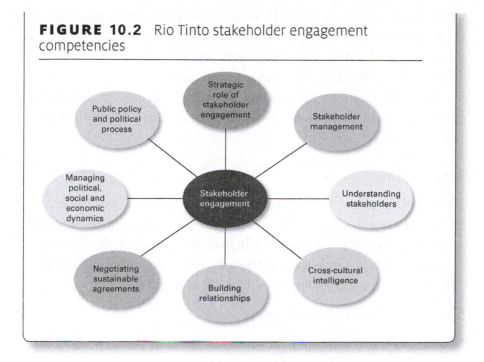

Online learning

Online learning is a good tool for awareness raising and for providing information to teams. PQ should feature in induction packages and other tailored online courses.

Using the intranet to feature news of cross-sector partnerships gives employees a feel for the innovative and valuable work going on across the organization. Sharing learning and experiences from diverse partnerships encourages others to think more creatively. For example, inviting partners and other stakeholders to contribute podcasts where they share their perspectives on what works and what doesn't opens up thinking and debate across the organization.

Coaching

Individuals in roles with a high or medium PQ relevance who need to acquire PQ capability quickly and are too senior to attend a generic leadership programme are most likely to respond best to tailored

PQ coaching. Coaches should understand PQ both in terms of the context and how to apply it. Both Valerie and Gerry are qualified coaches experienced in working with senior leaders. You can book PQ coaching direct at www.pqleadership.com.

If you are interested in developing the PQ capability of your existing coaches, workshops to familiarize existing coaches with PQ are also available.

Mentoring

Mentors should be senior leaders who have demonstrated PQ leadership and are able to share their experiences with individuals developing their own PQ. Running facilitated sessions with these mentors to share ideas, experience and learning with each other will prepare them better for supporting their individual mentees.

Assignments/secondments

Some individuals will show potential for PQ through their attitudes and behaviours but may lack experience of leading or working on complex projects, or of working across cultures. Using assignments to bring people on is not new. PQ should be treated in the same way as other disciplines that require structured development. Those with potential to be senior leaders should be directed to specific assignments to enable them to develop their PQ skills and experience.

Others may have strong credentials in visionary thinking, focus, rigour and getting things done, but lack sufficient empathy to build trusting relationships. Working on secondment with a cross-sector partner offers another way to understand their issues from 'the inside out'. Bringing the learning and insights back into the organization for work on future projects helps the individual compensate for any gaps. Ideally the secondment might be accompanied by some support on developing empathy from an internal or external coach to make a powerful learning experience.

Some organizations have invested resources in managing assignments and secondments to develop their staff. Others have process that focus on administration rather than finding the best fit of people to assignments. If you are in the latter category (you'll be in the majority), take the time to work out how to do it well and make sure it's resourced effectively. Finding the right assignments and secondments can be tricky. Too often it doesn't happen because the people running the process don't have the relationships to broker the assignment or secondment. And the people who do – often those in the operational areas – are not involved in the process.

Recruitment and selection

Recruitment or selection for roles with a high or medium-level PQ relevance should include testing for PQ capacity. Recruiters should be familiar with the PQ indicators and ask candidates for evidence of how they have demonstrated them.

Assessment centres for employee selection and/or internal promotion into roles with high/medium PQ relevance should include exercises that test PQ facets and indicators. The core areas to test are:

- ability to interact effectively in a shared power context – covering PQ facets empathy with purpose, power and versatility;
- ability to think conceptually and relate immediate events and actions to the future vision;
- understanding of the machinery of delivery through multiple layers of partners and stakeholders;
- commitment to ethical standards and integrity;
- an open and creative approach to working inclusively with a broad range of stakeholders.

Performance management

Paying attention to how leaders demonstrate PQ helps identify and reward good practice and offers an opportunity to provide additional support when it is needed. Using the organization's performance management system to do this formalizes the activity and provides the mechanism for delivery.

Performance appraisal processes should include review of both what leaders achieve and how they do it. Using the PQ framework helps leaders review their own performance and gives their managers an opportunity to identify any gaps between current performance and desired future performance. Once the gaps are known, they can inform personal development activity in the next period.

Further resources

We offer a range of materials and other resources to support you with implementing PQ. To find out more, please go to **www.pqleadership.com**. If you don't see what you are looking for, then please contact us direct. Our contact details are on the website.

Annex: The leadership challenge

You may be wondering whether PQ is relevant for you and your organization, or you may want to engage others in thinking about how you have adapted to a shared power world. If so, take a moment to pause and reflect on where you are right now. The following light-touch leadership challenge might be helpful. It is best to do this with a group of people to generate new thinking and benefit from a broad range of experiences.

The following questions might help you figure out whether you need to make changes. You should interpret the term 'partners' as meaning any other organization, whether in business, government or non-profit.

The challenge is a set of high-level questions that covers context, attitudes, values and infrastructure.

Challenge One: On a Post-it note, consider the changes in your environment and reflect on whether the traditional suite of leadership skills that worked in the later part of the 20th century fit the second decade of the 21st century. What is the difference in the challenges you and your organization face? Are you having a positive effect in the communities in which you operate? How are you perceived by the community, by your stakeholders, by wider society? Do you need to change the way you do things? And why? What changes do you need to make in the short term and the long term?

Challenge Two: Do you believe that you can achieve your objectives alone? If not, what changes are needed to help you work together more effectively with others? How do you build strategies that deliver mutual benefits for yourself and existing or future partners? Who are the right partners?

Challenge Three: Are you missing out on opportunities that you could use to further your goals if you had new partners or a different relationship with existing partners? Have you got effective relationships with the partners that might be able to mitigate risks for you? How will you build the types of relationships you need?

Challenge Four: Consider your and your organization's attitudes and behaviours to partners and potential partners. Opening questions you might ask are:

- Do we speak the same language? (ie how well do you understand and respect each other?)
- Do we understand what each other wants to achieve?
- Do we know how to build effective relationships?
- Do we know what we want from them?
- Do we truly know what they want from us?

Challenge Five: This goes deeper. What are the cultural and values issues that need to be addressed in your organization and with your partners?
Opening questions include:

- How much alignment is there between our values?

- Do we have trust?
- Do we understand the differences in our values and how that plays out?
- Do we have enough humility to work towards shared aims?
- Do we have enough curiosity to get the best from others?
- Are we contributing to wider society?
- Could we do more?
- How would that feel?

Challenge Six: This is about your infrastructure. Opening questions include:

- Do we have enough people with the skills required to lead in this way?
- Do we have the processes that we need?
- Do we have the right mix of expertise and advice available to us?
- How do we expand capability?

Looking ahead

11

Change is afoot. The drivers for change discussed in earlier chapters are forcing it. The world is shrinking. Globalization, complex societal challenges, changes in the environment, population, wealth and technology mean that the world is becoming more interdependent. Technology is connecting citizens across the world. Information that was once only known to a few is becoming visible to almost all. Business, government and society are drawn closer together by the reality of shared power. No one organization is in single control of its destiny.

What is changing? A global movement is emerging that believes in business, government and society working together across sectors and national boundaries to deliver profit, growth and societal benefit.

The roll call of supporters is impressive. It ranges across business leaders, political leaders, non-profit leaders and thought leaders, some of whom are referenced in this book. We have no doubt that we have captured only some of the pioneers. There are more stories emerging every day.

These leaders are advocating and role-modelling cross-sector and cross-cultural working to deliver profit, growth and a better world for people to live in, now and in the future. The next challenge is to escalate the number of leaders working in this way. We believe that most leaders and their employees are attracted by leadership that balances profit and growth with long-term benefit for society. Scaling up depends on finding ways to empower leaders in all sectors to do this by working in a politically intelligent way.

Explaining and defining political intelligence is our contribution to help leaders do this. The PQ model is both wide-ranging – covering behaviours, skills and processes – and firmly based in the practice of successful leaders. It prompts leaders to think and act in ways that will deliver success for their interests and the interests of everyone else.

What is the incentive for leaders to change?

We should all ask ourselves – what is the alternative? A world where business makes profit at the expense of the vulnerable and future generations? A world where governments make little progress on the big long-term challenges and focus only on short-term populist measures? A world where social media is exploited by the intolerant? A world where no one's children eat fresh fish?

Business leaders should ask – what if I don't change? Will consumers buy from competitors because they doubt the character of my company?

Governments should ask – what if I don't change? Will citizens seek information from others to tell them what is happening and to allow them to engage in the debate, for example through leaks?

Non-profits should ask – what if I don't change? Will donors find alternative ways of supporting others?

Very few people want these outcomes. So moving to a new leadership model that fits the challenges of our age is supported by the people mentioned in this book. They recognize that it's by working together across sectors and national boundaries that we can find innovative, long-term solutions to society's biggest problems. They emphasize the importance of an ethical and transparent approach that includes and involves people and secures their understanding and support.

We believe the future needs more leaders who understand that integral to their leadership role is helping their community and society to solve their biggest challenges. Society craves leaders who create and shape a better future; who stretch their own imaginations and trigger the imaginations of others.

Shaping that future when power is shared relies on: empathy with both individuals and humanity; building strong and trusted relationships with key partners and stakeholders; the courage and conviction to do what is necessary while persuading others to join in; and telling a story that helps everyone understand the balance between the needs of society and business, the global community and nation states, the future and the present.

How do we move forward?

We hope to see:

- more leaders embracing their responsibility towards their communities and wider society while maintaining their focus on delivery of results;

- more leaders working across sector, cultural and international divides to find long term and sustainable solutions that deliver profit, growth and societal benefits;

- business bringing its innovation and delivery skills to the work of governments and NGOs;

- governments working openly and inclusively with business and wider society to broaden policy thinking, also more emphasis on developing leaders with multilateral skills;

- more transparency and engagement with society in the non-profit sector;

- organizations developing PQ skills among their leaders and aspiring leaders;

- executive education mainstreaming the importance of delivering profit, growth and benefits for society in all leadership training, and with more focus on the PQ behaviours needed to work in a shared power world;

- more research on developing politically intelligent leadership to help leaders adapt to changes in the global environment and technology;

- more research and exploitation of technology to support leaders' efforts to provide long term, sustainable and ethical solutions to societal problems.

Just because we cannot see clearly the end of the road, that is no reason for not setting out on this essential journey. On the contrary, great change dominates the world, and unless we move with change we will become its victims.

Robert F Kennedy

REFERENCES

Achi, Z (2010) Balancing Wealth and Public Good: An interview with the COO of Abu Dhabi's Development Corporation, *McKinsey Quarterly*, September

Adams, T (2008) Our Man in Africa, *The Observer*, 11 May

Ahtisaari, M and Eiermann, M (2013) We Must Have the Courage to Defend Our Values, *The European* [online] http://www.theeuropean-magazine.com/martti-ahtisaari--2/6560-europe-and-the-world

Archbishop of Canterbury's toast at The Lord Mayor of London's Reception (2013) [online] http://www.archbishopofcanterbury.org/articles.php/5015/archbishop-of-canterburys-toast-at-the-lord-mayor-of-londons-reception

Barnard, A and Parker C (2012) *Campaign It! Achieving success through communication*, Kogan Page, London

Bennet, J (2012) The Bloomberg Way, *The Atlantic* [online] http://www.theatlantic.com/magazine/archive/2012/11/the-bloomberg-way/309136/

Berggruen, N and Gardels, N (2013) *Intelligent Governance for the 21st Century*, Polity Press, Cambridge

BG Approach to stakeholders [online]. www.bg-group.com

Blair, T (2011) Speech: Rethinking Leadership for Development [online] http://www.tonyblairoffice.org/speeches/entry/tony-blair-speech-rethinking-leadership-for-development/

Blair, T (2013) Address to the 5th Israeli Presidential Conference in Jerusalem [online] www.quartetrep.org

Branson, R Top 20 Inspirational Insights [online] http://www.virgin.com/entrepreneur/richard-bransons-top-20-virgin-inspirational-insights

Browne, Lord and Nuttall, R (March 2013) Beyond Corporate Responsibility: Integrated external engagement [online] http://www.mckinsey.com/insights/strategy/beyond_corporate_social_responsibility_integrated_external_engagement

Business Ethics Briefing (2012) Anti Bribery and Corruption Standards and Frameworks. Institute of Business Ethics, October

Cameron, D (2012) Speech to Business in the Community charity, www.gov.uk/government/speeches/businessinthecommunity

Charity Commission (2012) Public Trust and Confidence in Charities: Analysis of findings based on IPSOS MORI study 29 June 2012 [online] www.charitycommission.org.uk

Cheng, R and Spenley, K (2012) Sporting partnerships: Dubai sponsors Chinese table tennis team [online] www.vision.ae

Christenson, CM (2012) A Capitalist's Dilemma, *New York Times* 3 November [online] http://www.nytimes.com/2012/11/04/business/a-capitalists-dilemma-whoever-becomes-president.html

Clinton, B (2000) Speech: Eighth State of the Union Address [Online]. www.wikisource.org

Clinton, B (2012) Transcript of President Obama nomination speech, *New York Times* [online] http://www.nytimes.com/2012/09/05/us/politics/transcript-of-bill-clintons-speech-to-the-democratic-national-convention.html

Covey, S M R (2006) *The Speed of Trust: The one thing that changes everything,* Freepress, New York

Denning, S (2011) *The Leader's Guide to Storytelling*, Jossey-Bass, San Francisco

Dionisio, J M (2012) The Centerpiece of Trust: Treating ethics as a holistic value to the organization, *Ethisphere Qtr* 2/2012

Durando, J (2010) BP's Tony Hayward – 'I'd like my life back', *USA Today*, 1 June [online] www.usatoday.com

Edelman Trust Barometer (2013/2012/2011) [online] www.trust .edelman.com

Edemariam, A (2010) Mary Robinson: 'I feel a terrible sense of urgency'. *The Guardian*, 13 March

The Elders [online] www.theelders.org

Ernst and Young (2013) Global Report – Turn risks and opportunities into results: exploring the top 10 risks and opportunities for global organisations [online] http://www.ey.com/GL/en/Services/Advisory/Turn-risks-and-opportunities-into-results-2013---CFO-Report

Fisk, P (2010) *People, Planet, Profit*, Kogan Page, London

Gates, B (2013) Annual Letter *Bill and Melinda Gates Foundation* [online] www.annualletter.gatesfoundation.org

Goleman, D (1998) What Makes a Leader: Leadership insights, *Harvard Business Review* [online] www.hbr.com

Goleman, D (2011) Are Women More Emotionally Intelligent Than Men? *Psychology Today* [online] http://www.psychologytoday.com/blog/the-brain-and-emotional-intelligence/201104/are-women-more-emotionally-intelligent-men

Harris Polls (2013/2012/2011) [online] www.harrisinteractives.com

Helsby, N and Ungless, J (2011) The Changing Face of Public Affairs [online] http://www.watsonhelsby.co.uk/assets/files/The%20Changing%20Face%20of%20Public%20Affairs%20(2012).pdf

Huston, L and Munoz, T (2013) The Open Innovation Business Model [online] www.innovationexcellence.com/blog/20013/08/12

Ibrahim, Mo (2009) Interview with BBC World Services Africa: Mo Ibrahim's Mobile Revolution [online] http://news.bbc.co.uk/1/hi/world/africa/8309396.stm

Kleiner, A (2003) *Who Really Matters: The core group theory of power, privilege and success*, Doubleday, Random House Inc, USA

Krznaric, R (2012) The Six Habits of Highly Empathetic People [online] http://greatergood.berkeley.edu/article/item/six_habits_of_highly_empathic_people1

Liveris, A N (2013) Building The Future, *Chemical and Engineering News*, 1 July

LSE Growth Commission (2013) Investing for Prosperity: Skills, infrastructure and innovation report [online] http://www.lse.ac.uk/researchAndExpertise/units/growthCommission/documents/pdf/LSEGC-Report.pdf

Mahbubani, K (2013) *The Great Convergence*, Public Affairs, New York

Myers-Briggs Type Inventory [online] www.myersbriggs.org

Naim, M (2013) *The End of Power*, Basic Books, New York

Nakagawa, D and Moyo, D (2012) China is the Only Country With a Plan to Secure Scarce Global Resources, *The Christian Scientist Monitor* [online] http://www.csmonitor.com/Commentary/Global-Viewpoint/2012/1121/China-is-the-only-country-with-a-plan-to-secure-scarce-global-resources

National Commision on the BP Deepwater Horizon Oil Spill and Offshore Drilling (2011). Deep water – The Gulf Oil Disaster and future of offshore drilling [online] s3.amazonaws.com/pdf-final/DEEPWATER_reporttothepresident_FINAL.pdf

Nye, J S (2006) Seminar Harvard University: Soft Power, Hard Power and Leadership [online] http://www.hks.harvard.edu/netgov/files/talks/docs/11_06_06_seminar_Nye_HP_SP_Leadership.pdf

O'Donnell, Lord G (2013) The Warwick Policy Lab Will Triumph Where Ministers Struggle, *The Guardian*, 16 July

OECD (2012) Looking to 2060: long-term global growth prospects

The Official Report of the Fukushima Nuclear Accident Independent Investigation Commission. Executive Summary (2012) http://www.nirs.org/fukushima/naiic_report.pdf

Oliner Empathy Study, Greatergood e-newsletter, *University of California*, [online] http://greatergood.berkeley.edu/topic/empathy/definition

Oliver, J (2010) speech, Teach Every Child About Food [online] http://www.ted.com/talks/jamie_oliver.html

Pirson, M and Malhotra, D (2007) What Matters to Whom: Managing trust across multiple stakeholder groups, The Hauser Center for non-profit organisations, Harvard University

Porter, M and Kramer, M (2011) Creating Shared Value, *Harvard Business Review*, January

Powell, A (2013) Billionaire Patrice Motsepe Joins Club of African Philanthropists, *Voice of America* [online] www.voanews.com

Powell, General C (2012) *It Worked for Me: In life and leadership*, Harper Collins, New York

Powell, J (2011) *The New Machiavelli: How to wield power in the modern world*, Vintage, London

Power Africa [online] http://www.standardchartered.com/en/news-and-media/news/africa/2013-07-01-USD2bn-committed-to-Power-Africa.html

Putting People and Planet First [online] www.bteam.org

PwC (2013) 16th Annual Global CEO Survey: Dealing with disruption – Adapting to survive and thrive [online] www.pwc.com/ceosurvey

Radjou, N, Kaipa, P and Ahuja, S (2011) India's Decade of Collaboration [online] Blog.hbr.org/2011/05

Raikes, J (2013) Blogs Impatient Optimists Bill and Melinda Gates Foundation

Regan T and Branson R (March 2013) How Branson Enjoys His Success Adventures Interview on Bloomberg TV [online] www.bloomberg.com/video

Report on Bill Gates Speech to National Press Club (2013) ABC News [online] www.abc.net.au/news

Robinson, M (2013a) Interview with Kirsty Young, Desert Island Discs, BBC Radio 4, 28 July 2013 [online] http://www.bbc.co.uk/radio4/features/desert-island-discs/castaway/80b5d545#b037gm1f

Robinson, M (2013b) What makes us human? Jeremy Vine Radio 2 [podcast] http://downloads.bbc.co.uk/podcasts/radio2/human/human_20130605-1456c.mp3

Rose, C (2013) PBS: The Charlie Rose show – interview with Bono [online] www.one.org

Sandberg, S (2013) *Lean In: Women, work and the will to lead*, Random House, New York

Save the Children (2012) Policy Brief November 2012. Shared Value: how can large businesses contribute to the post-2015 agenda [online] www.savethechildren.org.uk

Simon-Thomas, E (2007) The Greater Good, University of California, Berkeley [online] www.greatergood.berkeley.edu

Standard Chartered Bank Annual Report 2012, Group Chief Executives Review. [online] http://www.standardchartered.com/en/resources/global-en/pdf/annual_reports/Standard_Chartered_Annual_Report_2012.pdf

Steingart, P and Schmitz, G P (2009) 'Is it pointless to talk to Al Quaida?' Interview with Professor Joseph Nye on Hard and Soft Power, Spiegel Online International. www.spiegel.de/international

Swartz, J (2012) Ebay founder, a philanthropic powerhouse, *USA Today*, 14 February

Topham, G (2012) West Coast Rail Petition Calls for Franchise to be Reconsidered, *The Guardian*, 24 August, www.guardian.com

Trompenaars, F and Hampden-Turner, C (1998) *Riding the Waves of Culture: Understanding diversity in global business,* 2nd edn, McGraw-Hill, USA

Virgin Atlantic sustainable aviation: LanzaTech story (2013) [online] www.virginatlantic.com and www.yourindustrynews.com

Wilton Park Conference Report WP1218 (2013) Resources: Trends and future challenges for states and regions – towards 2030 [online] https://www.wiltonpark.org.uk/conference/wp1218/

FURTHER READING

Christenson, C M (1997) *The Innovator's Dilemma: The revolutionary book that will change the way you do business*, Harvard Business School Press (Reprinted 2011 by Harper Collins, New York)

Collins, J C and Porras, J I (1996) Building your company's vision, *Harvard Business Review*

Goleman, D (1996) *Emotional Intelligence: why it can matter more than IQ*, Bloomsbury Publishing, London

Grinder, M (2010) *Charisma: The art of relationships*, Michael Grinder and Associates

Hersey, P and Blanchard , K, The Centre for Leadership Studies [online] www.situational.com

Jackson, P Z and McKergow, M (2002) *The Solutions Focus: the Simple way to Positive Change*, Nicholas Brearley, London.

Jensen, R (2001) *The Dream Society: How the coming shift from information to imagination will transform your business*, Mc Graw-Hill, USA

Kouzes, J M and Posner, B Z (2011) *The Five Practices of Exemplary Leadership* (2nd edition) Pfeiffer, USA

McKeown, M (2012) *The Strategy Book*, Pearson, Harlow, UK

Porter, E H, The Strength Deployment Inventory [online] www.personalstrengths.co.uk

Scott, S (2003) *Fierce Conversations: Achieving success in work and in life, one conversation at a time*, Piatkus, London

Thomas, K W and Kilmann, R H, The Thomas-Kilmann Conflict Mode Instrument [online] www.ccp.com

Williams, M and Penman, D (2011) *Mindfulness: a practical guide to finding peace in a frantic world*, Piatkus, London

Zetter, L (2011) *Lobbying: The art of political persuasion* (2nd edition), Harriman House, Petersfield, UK

INDEX

NB: page numbers in *italic* indicate figures or tables